CW01433551

Girl's Guide to Puberty

7 Friendly Ways to Understand Body Changes, Feelings, and Friendships During Puberty

E.J. Rico

E.J. Rico

Dedication

For the girls who are still figuring it out —
the ones who look in the mirror and wonder if they're changing *too fast* or *not fast enough.*
This is for you.

For the ones who sometimes feel like they're growing in ten different directions at once —
who laugh too loud, cry for no reason, dream big, and sometimes just want to hide under the covers until it all makes sense.
You are *seen.* You are *enough.* You are *becoming.*

For every girl who's ever whispered, "Is this normal?" —
yes, it is. Every feeling, every question, every beautiful, awkward, uncomfortable part of this journey... it's all part of growing up. And you're doing it perfectly.

For the parents, teachcrs, mentors, and quiet heroes who guide with patience and love —
thank you for showing up. For listening when it's hard. For answering questions you never expected to hear.

You make the world a safer place for growth to happen.

And for my younger self —
the one who didn't always know where she fit,
who tried to be brave even when she felt unsure,
who learned that self-love isn't something you find
— it's something you *build,* one kind thought at a
time —
this is for you, too.

May every girl who opens this book feel a little less alone.
May she find her reflection in these pages — not the perfect, polished version, but the real one — messy, radiant, and full of life.

And may she always remember:
growing up isn't something to fear.
It's something to *celebrate.*

Epigraph

"You're not becoming someone new. You're finally meeting the person you were always meant to be."
— *E.J. Rico*

TABLE OF CONTENTS

Introduction

Welcome to Your Growing-Up Journey

The first time I noticed my body changing, I remember staring at the mirror, unsure of what was happening. My jeans fit differently. My skin felt more sensitive. I cried at small things one day and laughed uncontrollably the next. It was confusing — like someone had swapped my old self with a newer version I didn't fully recognize yet.

Maybe you've felt that way too. Maybe you've looked in the mirror and thought, *"Is this normal?"* or felt unsure when your feelings seem to change faster than the weather. One moment, you're laughing with friends, and the next, you feel like crying for no reason at all. That's okay. It's all part of growing up — part of the amazing, sometimes messy, but always meaningful journey called **puberty**.

Puberty can feel *big*. And it is. It's the time when your body, your emotions, and even your friendships start to grow in new directions. Sometimes it's exciting; sometimes it's awkward; and sometimes, it's just plain weird. But here's the truth: **you're not alone.** Every girl goes through this stage — even the ones who seem like they have it all figured out. Every confident, happy, grown woman you know has been right where you are now: curious, unsure, and changing in ways she didn't always understand.

That's why I wrote this book — to be your **friendly guide** through it all. Not like a teacher giving a lecture, but more like an older sister who's been there, made sense of it, and is here to walk beside you as you figure things out too.

In these pages, you'll learn to understand your body's incredible transformation — why it changes, how to take care of it, and how to feel proud of it instead of confused or embarrassed. You'll also get to know your emotions better, discovering that feelings like frustration, shyness, or mood swings aren't scary at all once you learn what they're trying to tell you. And most importantly, you'll find gentle ways to build **stronger, kinder friendships** — with your friends, your family, and most of all, with yourself.

This isn't a "how-to" book that tells you what to do. It's a **"let's figure this out together"** kind of book. You'll see that every chapter is a step — or as I like to call them, **friendly ways** — to help you grow from confusion into confidence. You'll discover how to care for your body, manage your emotions, and navigate the changes around you with more understanding and self-love.

As you read, take your time. Some parts might feel familiar; others might surprise you. You can write notes, highlight lines, or even pause to think about your own experiences. This is your space — your chance to understand, accept, and celebrate who you're becoming.

Growing up doesn't mean losing who you are. It means discovering new sides of yourself — stronger, braver, and more beautiful ones that have been waiting to shine. And while this journey might have a few awkward moments, it's also filled with laughter, learning, and the kind of growth that makes you realize just how special you are.

So take a deep breath, open your heart, and get ready to learn the **7 friendly ways** to love your body, understand your feelings, and build friendships that make growing up a little easier — and a lot more joyful.

Let's begin your journey together — one friendly step at a time.

<u>Chapter 1</u>

Understanding What's

Happening — Your Body's

Amazing Changes

The Science of Change: What Puberty Really Is

Imagine waking up one day and realizing that your favorite T-shirt doesn't fit the same way it used to. Your voice sounds a little different. Your skin looks new somehow. Maybe you're growing taller so fast it feels like your legs can't keep up. If you've noticed things like this happening, congratulations — your body is doing something incredible. It's growing up.

Puberty is one of life's biggest transformations. It's not something to fear; it's something to *understand*. Inside you, your body is following a natural plan that every girl in the world goes through, though never in exactly the same way.

Here's the big secret adults often forget to tell you: puberty isn't just about your body changing on the outside. It's about everything inside you learning to work together — your brain, your hormones, and your emotions — to help you become the amazing young woman you're meant to be.

Hormones are the little messengers behind all these changes. You can't see them, but they're like tiny text messages sent between your brain and your body, telling it, "Hey, it's time to grow." These hormones wake up around the time your brain decides it's ready. They tell your bones to stretch, your muscles to strengthen, and your body to prepare for new stages of life.

Sometimes these changes happen so slowly you hardly notice. Other times, it feels like everything is happening all at once — one day you're just you, and the next day you're a taller, curvier, moodier, hungrier version of yourself. That's all part of the plan, too.

The most important thing to remember is that **there's no exact right way to grow up.** Some girls start puberty earlier, and others later. Some grow fast, while others take their time. You might be the first in your friend group to notice changes, or the last — and either way, you're perfectly normal.

When you understand what's going on, you realize there's nothing strange or embarrassing about it. It's just your body becoming its strongest, healthiest, most beautiful version — the one that was always meant to bloom in its own time.

What Hormones Do and Why They Matter

Let's take a closer look at those little messengers — hormones. You've probably heard the word before, maybe whispered during health class or mentioned by adults with knowing smiles. But what are hormones, really?

Think of hormones as tiny helpers created by special parts of your body called glands. One of the most important is the pituitary gland, a small part in your brain that works like the boss of all your body's changes. When it's time, the pituitary gland sends out signals that say, "It's time to grow!"

These signals travel through your bloodstream and talk to other glands in your body — like the ovaries, which begin producing hormones called estrogen and progesterone. These two work together to shape many of the changes you'll see in yourself, from developing breasts to starting your period.

Hormones also affect your emotions. That's why you might feel extra sensitive or notice your moods shifting more quickly than before. It doesn't mean something is wrong — it just means your body and brain are working hard to stay balanced while you grow.

Here's something most girls find comforting to know: hormones don't stay wild forever. Once your body gets used to them, your moods and feelings will even out again. It's like learning to ride a bike — wobbly at first, but steady once you find your rhythm.

Understanding hormones helps take away the fear. Instead of thinking, *"Why am I like this?"* you can remind yourself, *"Oh, my body's just adjusting. I'm growing, and that's amazing."*

What Happens Inside: Growth, Periods, and Physical Changes

Now let's talk about what's actually happening *inside* your body — because it's fascinating, not frightening.

You're probably growing taller, maybe even feeling a little clumsy as your body catches up with itself. Your arms and legs might feel longer, and your clothes start fitting differently. This stage can feel awkward, but remember — every inch of growth is proof that your body is doing its job perfectly.

Breast development is often one of the first signs of puberty. It can feel strange at first, maybe even uncomfortable, but it's just your body preparing for adulthood in its own natural way. Some girls grow quickly, while others take months or years to fully develop. There's no "normal" pace — your body knows exactly what to do.

Then there's your period — a change that can feel big, mysterious, or even scary before it happens. But really,

It's just your body's way of saying everything is working beautifully. Each month, your uterus builds a soft lining that can nourish life someday. When it's not needed, your body simply releases it. That's what your period is — a natural, healthy rhythm that's unique to every girl.

When your first period arrives, it's okay to feel nervous or curious. You might wonder how to manage it or what products to use. The good news is that there are so many options now — pads, tampons, and even period underwear designed to keep you comfortable. And here's another secret: no one can tell when you're on your period unless you tell them. It's a private part of life that you'll quickly learn to handle like the capable, growing girl you are.

You might also notice hair growing in new places — under your arms, around your legs, and in your private area. That's another sign your hormones are doing their job. Everyone's different when it comes to how much hair grows or how quickly, and there's no rule about whether you should remove it. What matters is feeling clean, comfortable, and confident.

Your skin might also start acting up. Pimples, oiliness, or dryness are common, but temporary. Keeping your skin clean, drinking water, and getting enough rest can make a huge difference. Remember, even people you see online with "perfect" skin deal with breakouts — they just don't always show it.

Each change your body goes through — every curve, stretch, or new sensation — is proof of your strength and growth. It might not always feel glamorous, but it's part of your story, and it's something to be proud of.

Busting Myths About "What's Normal"

If you ever compare yourself to your friends, social media influencers, or even older girls you admire, it's easy to wonder, *"Am I normal?"* The short answer is yes — completely. The long answer is that **there's no single definition of normal.**

Some girls start their period at nine; others at thirteen. Some grow tall early; others stay petite longer. Bodies don't grow in sync, and that's what makes every one of them beautiful.

One of the biggest myths is that puberty should look the same for everyone. It doesn't. Just like flowers bloom in their own season, your body grows at its own perfect pace. Comparing yourself to others only steals the joy of discovering how uniquely wonderful you are.

Another myth is that puberty should be embarrassing. It's not. Talking about your body doesn't make you weird; it makes you wise. Learning about puberty isn't about shame — it's about understanding and celebrating what makes you, *you*.

And finally, don't believe the myth that confidence comes *after* puberty — when you're "finished growing." Confidence grows *with* you. It builds every time you choose to accept your body, treat yourself kindly, and learn something new about who you're becoming.

Your body is doing one of the most beautiful things it will ever do: changing, growing, and preparing you for the next chapter of your life. Every stretch mark, every mood swing, every new discovery is part of the masterpiece that is *you*.

So the next time you catch yourself in the mirror, don't just see the changes. See the strength. See the girl who's learning, growing, and stepping into her power — one amazing change at a time.

Loving the Skin You're In

It was a sunny Saturday morning when Mia stood in front of her mirror, frowning at her reflection. Her hair seemed frizzier than usual, her skin wasn't as clear as the girl she'd seen on TikTok, and her favorite jeans suddenly felt snug around her hips. "Why can't I look normal?" she whispered to herself.

Maybe you've felt like Mia before — standing in front of a mirror, wondering if you measure up. You notice a new curve, a pimple that wasn't there yesterday, or a body part that feels out of proportion. It's easy to think that everyone else looks perfect, especially when social media filters make it seem that way. But here's the truth that even adults sometimes forget: **your body isn't supposed to look like anyone else's.** It's supposed to look like *yours*.

Your body tells the story of you — your laughter, your adventures, the food you love, the hugs you've given, the nights you've stayed up reading or dreaming. It's the home you'll live in for your entire life. And right now, it's changing, growing, and becoming something stronger and more beautiful than ever before.

Learning to love your body doesn't happen overnight. It's something you *practice*. It's not about pretending you're perfect — it's about realizing that you were never meant to be perfect in the first place. You were meant to be real, and real is always more beautiful.

Learning to Appreciate Your Body's Uniqueness

Let's be honest: growing up in a world full of selfies, filters, and "perfect" pictures can make anyone feel unsure. You scroll through social media and see people with flawless skin, shiny hair, and perfect smiles — and it's easy to think, *I wish I looked like that.*

But what most people don't realize is that those pictures are often edited or filtered. Even the people you see online have days when they feel insecure. What matters most isn't how you look in a picture — it's how you *feel* in your own skin.

Every body is different — and that's something to celebrate. Some girls have curly hair that seems to dance in the sunlight; others have straight hair that shines like silk. Some have freckles sprinkled like stars across their cheeks, while others have smooth, deep skin that glows naturally. Some grow taller early; others stay smaller longer. There's no single version of "beautiful," because beauty doesn't come in one shape, size, or color.

When you start noticing what makes your body unique — the shape of your smile, the tone of your voice, the sparkle in your eyes when you laugh — you begin to see yourself differently. Instead of focusing on what you *don't* like, you begin to appreciate what makes you *you*.

It helps to remember that your body is working hard for you every single day. Your heart beats without being told. Your lungs breathe while you sleep. Your legs carry you to school, to dance class, to your best friend's house. Your hands draw, write, play, and hold the people you love. When you think about it, your body is doing something miraculous — it's helping you live your life.

So the next time you stand in front of a mirror, instead of asking, *"What's wrong with me?"* try whispering, *"Thank you, body, for all the things you do for me."* That small shift in thinking — from criticism to gratitude — is how body confidence begins.

Self-Care Basics for Hygiene, Health, and Comfort

Loving your body also means *taking care* of it — not because you have to, but because you deserve to. Self-care isn't about being fancy or spending a lot of money. It's about showing your body kindness in small, simple ways.

Start with the basics: keeping clean. As your body changes, it begins to produce more sweat and oil. That's completely normal — it's just your body's way of growing up. Taking a shower regularly, washing your hair when it feels greasy, and changing your clothes daily can help you feel fresh and confident. Using deodorant after bathing keeps you smelling good and feeling comfortable throughout the day.

You'll also notice that your skin might start acting differently. Maybe it gets oilier, or you get small pimples that make you want to hide your face. Don't worry — this happens to almost everyone during puberty. The best thing you can do is wash your face gently with a mild cleanser and avoid scrubbing too hard. Harsh products often make things worse. Drink water, eat fruits and vegetables, and get enough sleep — your skin will thank you.

And then there's your period. If you've started menstruating, you already know it's a big change. If you haven't yet, it's okay — it'll happen when your body's ready. Periods are a natural, healthy part of growing up. When your period arrives, using pads or period underwear can help you stay clean and comfortable. Remember to change them regularly and carry extras when you go out — just in case.

Good hygiene is also about feeling comfortable in your body, not just clean. Wear clothes that make you feel good, not just ones that are trendy. Choose cotton underwear that lets your skin breathe. Brush your teeth twice a day, and don't forget to floss. Take care of your hair — not to look "perfect," but to feel fresh and confident.

And yes, rest is part of self-care, too. Your body is doing so much growing during puberty that sleep becomes extra important. Aim for enough hours every night so you can wake up feeling refreshed and ready to take on your day.

When you care for your body in small, gentle ways, you're telling yourself, *"I matter."* That simple truth — that you deserve care — is what builds real confidence from the inside out.

Positive Self-Talk and Body Image Building

The words you speak to yourself are powerful. They can lift you up — or tear you down.

Think about how you talk to your friends. If your best friend said, "I hate how I look," you'd probably rush to remind her of all the things that make her special. You'd tell her she's beautiful, funny, kind, and strong. Now imagine if you talked to yourself that same way.

When you look in the mirror, it's easy to focus on what you wish were different — your nose, your hair, your size. But what if, instead, you looked for what you love? Try saying things like, *"I love my smile."* or *"I'm proud of how strong my legs are."* You don't have to believe it right away — just saying it starts to change the way your brain sees you.

The more you practice positive self-talk, the easier it becomes. And over time, you'll notice something incredible: you'll start to believe it.

Your body hears everything your mind says. When you feed it kindness, it responds with confidence. When you practice gratitude, it rewards you with peace. And when you remind yourself that your worth isn't measured by your reflection, you become unstoppable.

Body image isn't about comparing yourself to anyone else — it's about learning to *see yourself fully.* Every girl has moments when she doesn't feel confident, but what matters most is what you do next. Will you choose to criticize yourself, or will you choose compassion?

The truth is, your body is your lifelong teammate. It will carry you through every adventure, every goal, and every dream. It deserves love — not because it's perfect, but because it's yours.

Loving the skin you're in isn't just a phrase — it's a promise to yourself. A promise that no matter how your body changes, you'll treat it with respect, kindness, and care. It's about standing in front of the mirror, smiling softly, and knowing that the girl looking back at you is learning, growing, and becoming someone extraordinary.

Because she is.
Because you are.

The Power of Knowing

When Ella first learned that puberty meant getting her period, she felt a strange mix of curiosity and panic. She'd heard whispers from her classmates — "It's so gross," one said. "It hurts so bad," said another. For days, she dreaded what was coming, imagining something terrible. Then one evening, her older sister sat her down and explained what really happens — calmly, simply, and honestly.

"It's not scary," her sister said. "It's just your body doing what it's meant to do. Once you understand it, it's actually pretty amazing."

That conversation changed everything for Ella. She realized that what made puberty feel frightening wasn't the change itself — it was not *knowing* what was happening. Once she understood her body's rhythm and purpose, the fear started to fade, and something else took its place: confidence.

That's the real secret of growing up — the **power of knowing.** The more you understand about your body, your emotions, and the changes ahead, the stronger you feel. Knowledge doesn't just fill your brain; it gives you calm, courage, and control.

Think about the first time you walked into a dark room. Before you turned on the light, it felt eerie and uncertain. But once you flipped the switch, everything made sense. Puberty is the same way. The light switch is knowledge. When you know what's happening, you see that nothing is as scary as it first seemed.

Sometimes adults forget to explain things, or they assume you already know. That's why this chapter exists — to give you that light switch, so you can see clearly, understand deeply, and feel ready for what's ahead.

Common Questions Girls Ask About Puberty (With Honest Answers)

Puberty brings a lot of questions, and that's perfectly normal. Asking means you care enough to learn — and learning means you're already growing wiser. Here are some of the most common questions girls your age ask, with honest, judgment-free answers you deserve to hear.

One of the biggest questions girls have is, *"When will I start my period?"* The truth? There's no exact time. Some girls start around age nine, others around thirteen, and both are completely normal. Your body decides when it's ready. Usually, you'll notice a few signs before it happens — maybe breast growth, mood changes, or a little discharge in your underwear. Those are your body's friendly hints that it's preparing.

Another question that often comes up is, *"Will it hurt?"* Your period can cause mild cramps or discomfort, but it's rarely unbearable. Sometimes it feels like a soft squeeze in your lower belly, and a warm compress, gentle exercise, or rest can make it better. Over time, you'll learn what helps your body feel comfortable. And remember — it's not punishment or something to be ashamed of. It's your body's monthly reminder that it's healthy and doing exactly what it's supposed to do.

Then there's the classic, *"Why am I so emotional?"* You might laugh one minute and feel teary the next. It doesn't mean you're being dramatic; it means your hormones are balancing themselves while your brain learns how to respond. Puberty affects emotions because your body is growing and your feelings are learning to stretch, too. Talking about your emotions — even when it feels awkward — helps you handle them better.

Many girls also whisper to themselves, *"Is my body normal?"* And the answer is always yes. Everyone grows at a different pace. Maybe your chest is developing before your friends', or maybe it hasn't started yet. Maybe your legs are long and your arms are thin, or your hips are starting to curve. No matter what, you're normal. There is no "right" timeline or body shape.

Sometimes you might worry about sweat, body odor, or pimples. These changes happen because your sweat glands and skin are becoming more active. It's part of your body adjusting to its new stage. Showering regularly, using deodorant, and washing your face gently can help you feel fresh and confident.

And of course, one of the most private questions of all: *"Is it okay to feel embarrassed about my body?"* Absolutely. Everyone feels shy or awkward sometimes. But as you understand what's happening, that embarrassment fades and pride takes its place. You'll realize that growing up doesn't make you strange — it makes you strong.

Every question you ask, every new thing you learn, builds your confidence. That's the beauty of knowledge: it replaces fear with understanding. When you know the truth about your body, you can handle anything it throws your way — with grace, courage, and even a little bit of humor.

Journaling Prompts for Self-Reflection

Sometimes the best way to understand yourself is to talk to the one person who knows you best — *you.* Journaling is one of the most powerful tools for self-reflection during puberty. Writing down your thoughts helps you make sense of what's going on in your heart and mind. It's a private, judgment-free space to ask questions, celebrate wins, and release worries.

Imagine your journal as your closest friend — one who listens without interrupting and never laughs at your questions. You can write about anything: your day, your feelings, your changes, your friendships. When you put your thoughts on paper, they stop swirling around in your head and start to make sense.

You don't have to write perfectly. You don't even have to write a lot. Just be honest. Your words don't have to sound fancy or wise — they just have to be yours.

Start by writing about how you feel about growing up. Are you excited? Nervous? Curious? There's no wrong answer. Describe what you notice in your body — maybe you feel stronger, or taller, or different somehow. Then, explore your emotions. Have your moods been shifting? Are you feeling more sensitive or creative lately? All of these are important clues about how you're changing.

Journaling can also help when you're confused or upset. Let's say you have a bad day and feel like no one understands you. Instead of keeping those feelings bottled up, write them down. When you see them on paper, they don't feel so heavy. Often, you'll realize that what seemed impossible to handle a few hours ago now feels manageable.

You can even use your journal to write letters to your future self. Imagine the confident, happy young woman you're becoming and tell her what you're learning now. Maybe write about how you handled your first period, your first time standing up for yourself, or the first day you truly liked what you saw in the mirror. These moments might seem small, but someday, when you look back, you'll see how big they really were.

If you're not a fan of writing paragraphs, that's okay too. Doodle your feelings. Write short phrases, song lyrics, or even a single word that captures how you feel. Your journal doesn't need rules; it only needs honesty.

What matters most is that you make time for it — even a few minutes before bed. Over time, you'll notice something magical: as you write, you begin to understand yourself better. You'll start to spot patterns — like when you tend to feel your best, what makes you happy, or what triggers your moods. That awareness gives you power. It helps you care for yourself with kindness instead of confusion.

Knowledge doesn't always come from books or teachers. Sometimes, it comes from listening to yourself. Every word you write becomes a piece of your story — proof that you're learning, growing, and becoming more self-aware each day.

The power of knowing isn't just about facts; it's about *understanding yourself*. When you know what's happening inside your body, you no longer have to guess or fear. When you ask questions and seek honest answers, you become more confident. And when you take time to write, reflect, and listen to your own thoughts, you build a kind of wisdom that will guide you far beyond puberty.

Knowledge lights the way — but you are the one walking it. Every bit you learn, every truth you uncover, makes you stronger, braver, and more beautifully you.

<u>Chapter 2</u>

Listening to Your Feelings —

Understanding Emotions

and Mood Swings

What's Going On Inside?

There was a time when Mia couldn't understand why she felt like crying over something as small as losing her favorite pen. It wasn't even a special pen—just blue and sparkly—but when it slipped out of her backpack and vanished, tears filled her eyes before she could stop them. The next minute, she was laughing at a funny meme her friend sent her. Then, out of nowhere, she felt irritated again, snapping at her little brother for humming too loudly.

If that sounds familiar, you're not alone. Puberty often feels like an emotional roller coaster—one moment you're soaring with excitement, and the next, you're plunging into frustration or sadness without warning. You might wonder, *Why am I like this? Why can't I control how I feel?* But here's the truth: there's nothing wrong with you. What you're feeling is exactly what growing up feels like on the inside.

During puberty, your body isn't the only thing changing—your brain and emotions are, too. Inside you, a lot of amazing and complicated things are happening. Your hormones (those tiny chemical messengers you learned about earlier) are now working overtime. They're not just telling your body to grow—they're also affecting your mood, your thoughts, and even how you see the world.

When hormones like estrogen and progesterone start flowing, they don't just change your physical body; they also talk directly to your brain. Think of it like this: hormones send messages to the parts of your brain that control emotions, like joy, anger, or sadness. Because your brain is still learning to balance all these signals, sometimes the messages get mixed up. That's why a small thing—like someone ignoring your text or a teacher's comment—can feel *huge* in the moment.

And guess what? That's completely normal.

When you feel like crying for no reason, it doesn't mean you're weak. When you get irritated more easily than before, it doesn't mean you're a bad person. It just means your body and brain are adjusting to all the new signals they're receiving. Your emotions might feel louder right now, but over time, they'll start to even out again.

It's also important to know that emotions themselves aren't bad. Many people grow up thinking they need to "control" or "hide" their feelings, but the truth is, emotions are messages. They're your body's way of helping you understand what's going on inside your heart and mind.

How Hormones Affect Moods and Emotions

Imagine your brain as a busy orchestra, with each instrument representing a different emotion. Happiness plays the flute, sadness strums the cello, anger beats the drum, and excitement plays the violin. When you were younger, your emotional orchestra played soft, simple songs. But now that puberty has begun, your hormones are like a new conductor—one who's still learning how to keep everyone in tune.

Sometimes the flute of happiness plays too loudly, and you feel unstoppable. Other times, the drums of anger take over, and every little thing seems annoying. Then suddenly, sadness's cello plays a quiet note, and you feel heavy or teary without knowing why. That's what hormonal changes can do.

You may notice mood swings—feeling cheerful one moment and frustrated the next. It might seem unpredictable, but it's really your brain adjusting to the new rhythm your hormones are creating. Over time, your "conductor" learns how to balance everything again, and your emotional music starts to flow more smoothly.

One reason puberty feels intense is because your emotional part of the brain (called the amygdala) develops faster than the part that helps you think calmly (the prefrontal cortex). That means sometimes, your emotions jump in before your logic does. You might cry before you understand why or say something you didn't mean. Everyone—yes, even adults—does this sometimes. The good news is that your brain is growing stronger every day. The more you understand what's happening, the easier it becomes to handle your feelings with kindness instead of confusion.

Why You Might Cry, Get Angry, or Feel Confused More Often

There are days when everything feels like *too much*. You might cry because you feel left out, even if your friends didn't mean to exclude you. Or you might get angry at your parents for asking about your day, even when they're just trying to help. Sometimes you'll feel fine one minute, then suddenly anxious or self-conscious the next. It's okay.

These emotional waves are a natural part of growing up. Crying helps your body release built-up tension—it's your body's reset button. Anger, on the other hand, is often a sign that something inside you feels unfair or out of control. And confusion? That usually means you're in the middle of figuring something out about yourself or the world.

Instead of judging these feelings, try to listen to them. What are they trying to tell you? Are you tired? Stressed? Feeling misunderstood? Sometimes the real reason behind your emotions isn't what's on the surface. You might cry over a small argument, but underneath, you're actually worried about fitting in. You might snap at your mom, but deep down, you're frustrated because you don't feel heard.

Learning to pause and ask, *"What's really going on?"* can turn emotions from chaos into clarity. The more curious you are about your feelings, the easier it becomes to handle them in healthy ways—like talking to someone you trust, taking deep breaths, or writing down your thoughts.

No one expects you to be happy all the time. In fact, if you never felt sadness or anger, you'd miss out on what those emotions can teach you. Sadness helps you understand what matters most. Anger reminds you to stand up for yourself. Even embarrassment can teach you humility and humor. Every emotion you feel has a purpose.

So the next time your feelings feel "too big," try to remember that they're not your enemies. They're guides—each one showing you a little more about who you are.

Emotions as Messengers, Not Enemies

Think of your emotions as text messages from your inner self. Each one carries a different message:

> Happiness says, "Keep going—you're doing something right."
>
> Anger says, "Something feels unfair; let's fix it."
>
> Sadness says, "You need care and comfort right now."
>
> Fear says, "Something feels uncertain; pay attention."

You wouldn't ignore a text from your best friend, right? So don't ignore messages from yourself, either.

When you treat your emotions like friends instead of problems, you start building emotional intelligence—a kind of wisdom that helps you understand yourself and others. You begin to see patterns: what makes you happy, what drains your energy, what helps you calm down. This awareness gives you the power to choose how you respond, instead of being swept away by feelings you don't understand.

Emotional awareness doesn't mean you'll never feel upset again—it means you'll start recognizing *why* you feel that way. You'll start noticing when your body tenses up, when your heart races, or when your stomach feels tight. Those physical signs are like emotional clues, telling you what needs your attention.

Some girls find it helpful to give their emotions names. You might think of your anger as a fiery dragon or your sadness as a gentle rain cloud. When you see them this way, they become less intimidating. You can talk to them, learn from them, and then let them pass when they're ready.

Remember, emotions aren't meant to be bottled up or ignored. When you try to hide them, they only grow stronger. But when you let them out—through talking, writing, drawing, or even crying—they lose their power to control you.

Listening to your feelings doesn't make you dramatic; it makes you wise. It helps you grow into someone who understands herself deeply, and that's one of the most powerful things any girl can learn.

Understanding your emotions is like learning a new language—the language of *you*. It takes time, patience, and practice. But once you learn to listen, you'll find that your feelings aren't scary at all. They're simply your body's way of saying, "Hey, I'm here. Let's figure this out together."

And that's the real magic of growing up—discovering that even when things feel messy, you already have everything you need inside you to handle it with strength, grace, and heart.

Tools for Emotional Balance

The first time Lila felt like her emotions were out of control, she was sitting in her room after an argument with her mom. Her chest felt tight, her throat heavy, and tears burned at the edge of her eyes. She didn't know if she was angry, sad, or both. She just knew she wanted the feeling to stop.

She grabbed her pillow and pressed it to her face, hoping that would help. But it didn't. So, without really thinking, she stood up, opened her window, and took a deep breath. The air was cool and sharp, like a soft reset button. She exhaled slowly, again and again, until her shoulders started to relax. The tightness in her chest softened. For the first time in a while, she could think clearly.

That's the power of emotional balance — it doesn't mean you never get upset; it means you learn how to *soothe yourself* when emotions get loud. Growing up brings so many new feelings that it can sometimes feel like you're being tossed around by invisible waves. But with a few gentle tools, you can learn how to find your calm again, no matter how stormy things get inside.

Simple Breathing, Grounding, and Mindfulness Techniques

Your breath is your built-in calm button. It's the one thing that's always with you, no matter where you are — at school, at home, or even during a stressful moment with friends. When you learn to use it, it becomes one of your strongest tools for peace.

Have you ever noticed how your breathing changes with your emotions? When you're nervous, your breaths get shorter. When you're relaxed, they slow down naturally. That's because your breath and your brain are connected — when one calms down, the other follows.

Here's something powerful to remember: the moment you stop to take a slow, deep breath, you're already helping your body and brain find balance again.

Imagine this: you're in class, and suddenly your teacher calls on you to read aloud. Your heart starts racing, your palms get sweaty, and your thoughts scatter like papers in the wind. In that moment, if you simply pause, inhale deeply through your nose, and exhale slowly through your mouth, you'll feel your heartbeat begin to settle. It's like telling your body, *"I'm safe. I can handle this."*

Grounding is another quiet trick that helps when your thoughts start to spin too fast. It means bringing your attention back to the present — to where you are, right now. You can do it anywhere: feel your feet pressing against the floor, notice the weight of your body in your chair, or listen for sounds around you — a bird outside, a soft hum, your own breath. These small things remind your brain that you're here, not lost in your worries.

Mindfulness takes grounding a step further. It's about noticing your feelings without judging them. Instead of thinking, *"I shouldn't feel angry,"* you simply think, *"I'm feeling angry right now."* That simple shift — naming your feeling instead of fighting it — gives you power over it. The feeling still exists, but it no longer controls you.

Practicing mindfulness doesn't require meditation mats or candles (though those are nice, too). It's something you can do while brushing your teeth, walking to school, or lying in bed. Just notice your breath, your body, your thoughts. You don't have to fix anything — you just have to notice.

The more you practice, the faster you'll find your way back to calm when things feel big or messy.

Journaling and Drawing Your Feelings

Sometimes, the best way to understand your feelings is to let them spill onto paper. Journaling is like having a private conversation with your own heart — one that doesn't judge, interrupt, or tell you you're overreacting.

You don't need to be a writer to keep a journal. You don't even have to write full sentences. Just grab a notebook, open a blank page, and let your thoughts flow. Some days it might look like a jumble of words: "I'm so mad!" or "Why do I feel weird today?" Other days, it might turn into a poem, a doodle, or a few lines about something that made you smile.

The magic isn't in how it looks — it's in what it *releases*. When you write or draw what you feel, you take the pressure off your heart. Suddenly, that confusing swirl of emotions becomes something you can see, something you can work through.

Some girls like to draw their emotions instead of writing about them. You could draw what "anger" looks like — maybe it's a fiery storm. Or what "happiness" feels like — maybe it's a sun with dancing rays. Art lets your feelings speak in colors and shapes when words don't quite fit.

Over time, journaling or drawing becomes a record of your growth. When you look back, you'll see how strong you've become, how much you've learned, and how many feelings you've already survived. Each page becomes proof that emotions don't stay forever — they pass, just like clouds moving through the sky.

Journaling also helps your brain organize itself. When you put thoughts into words or images, it's like untangling a knot — suddenly, everything feels clearer. And clarity gives you control.

If you ever feel like your emotions are "too much," grab a pen, a pencil, or even your favorite colored markers. Let your feelings have a voice. Once you do, you'll find they don't shout as loudly anymore.

How to Talk About Emotions with Parents or Friends

Talking about feelings can be hard, especially when you're not sure what to say. You might worry that your parents won't understand, or that your friends will think you're being dramatic. But sharing what's in your heart isn't a sign of weakness — it's a sign of courage.

Sometimes, adults forget what it feels like to be your age. They might seem too busy, or they might try to "fix" things right away when all you really want is for someone to listen. That's why it helps to start by saying something simple, like, "I'm not looking for advice right now — I just need to talk." You'd be surprised how much that changes the conversation.

When you open up about your emotions, you give others a chance to understand you better. It's like handing them a small map that says, *"Here's where I am right now — please meet me here."*

Talking to friends can help, too. True friends don't need you to pretend. They'll listen when you're upset, laugh with you when you're happy, and sometimes, just sit quietly beside you when words aren't enough. Friendship isn't about always being cheerful — it's about being real with each other.

If talking out loud feels uncomfortable, you can start small. Maybe send a message that says, "Hey, I've been feeling off lately," or write a note to someone you trust. You don't have to explain everything at once. You just have to take one brave step toward being honest.

And if you ever feel emotions that are too heavy — like sadness that doesn't go away, or anger that feels out of control — it's always okay to ask for help. Teachers, counselors, older siblings, or trusted adults are there for a reason. Asking for help doesn't mean you can't handle things. It means you *care enough about yourself* to reach out for support.

The more you practice talking about your emotions, the easier it becomes. Each time you do, you build stronger connections — not just with others, but with yourself.

There's a quiet kind of power in learning how to balance your emotions. It's not about being perfectly calm all the time — it's about knowing how to find your way back when life feels loud. It's about breathing through the storm, writing your truth, and reaching for the people who love you when you need them most.

And with every deep breath, every word written, and every brave conversation, you become more confident in the one person you'll always have — yourself.

Turning Feelings Into Strength

When Zoe first started noticing how easily she got upset, she thought something was wrong with her. One moment she'd be laughing with her best friend, and the next she'd be irritated for no reason. She couldn't explain why her heart sometimes felt heavy or why she suddenly wanted to cry during a movie she'd seen a dozen times.

But over time, something shifted. Zoe began to notice that her feelings weren't random. They were like clues — little messages telling her what she cared about most. When she felt jealous, it was because she wanted to belong. When she felt sad, it was because something mattered deeply to her. And when she felt happy, it reminded her of what filled her with joy.

That's when Zoe realized something powerful: **feelings aren't weaknesses — they're teachers.** They help us learn who we are, what we love, and how to understand others better.

Puberty doesn't just grow your body; it grows your *heart* too. Your emotions might feel more intense now, but that's because your empathy, compassion, and understanding are expanding right alongside them. You're learning to feel deeply — and that's one of the greatest strengths a person can have.

Learning From What You Feel

Think of your emotions as the weather inside you. Some days are calm and sunny, filled with laughter and lightness. Other days are stormy, full of thunder and rain. It's easy to wish away the storms, but they're not your enemies — they're what help things grow. Just like rain nourishes flowers, your feelings help you grow from the inside out.

When you feel something — anything — it's your body and mind trying to tell you something important. For example, when you feel angry, it's not just random frustration. It might be your heart saying, *"Something feels unfair."* When you feel anxious, your body is whispering, *"I'm worried about what might happen."* When you feel happy, it's your inner voice celebrating something good.

Once you start listening to what your emotions are trying to teach you, you begin to understand yourself on a whole new level. You start noticing patterns — like how certain situations always make you nervous or how helping someone always makes you feel proud. That awareness gives you the power to choose how to react.

It's okay if you don't always understand your feelings right away. Sometimes, you'll only figure them out later, when you have space to think. That's what growing emotional intelligence is all about — learning to pause, reflect, and respond with kindness toward yourself.

Try to see each emotion as a lesson, not a test. If you make a mistake — like snapping at your mom when you're stressed — you can always go back and say, "I'm sorry, I was just feeling overwhelmed." That moment of awareness doesn't make you weaker; it makes you wiser. It means you're paying attention to what's going on inside instead of letting your feelings control you.

Developing Empathy and Kindness

One of the most beautiful things that happens during puberty is that your capacity for empathy grows — even if it doesn't feel like it at first. Empathy means being able to understand what someone else is feeling, even if you're not in their shoes. It's like having emotional x-ray vision — you can sense when a friend is upset even if she's pretending to be fine.

When your own feelings become more complex, you naturally start noticing that everyone around you has feelings, too. You begin to realize that when someone is rude, it might be because they're having a hard day. Or when a friend goes quiet, it doesn't mean she's mad at you — maybe she's just tired or sad about something else.

The more you understand yourself, the more patient you become with others. That's what kindness really is — it's not about always being cheerful; it's about choosing compassion, even when it's hard.

Sometimes kindness means saying nothing, just sitting beside someone who needs company. Other times, it means standing up for someone who's being teased, even if your heart is racing. Kindness doesn't have to be big or dramatic — it just has to be real.

When you start to treat people with empathy, something amazing happens: you also start treating *yourself* with empathy. You begin to forgive yourself for mistakes, comfort yourself when you're upset, and speak to yourself with the same gentleness you give to others.

Imagine the world if everyone did that — if everyone took a moment to think, *"Maybe they're having a hard time,"* before reacting. You have the power to start that ripple. Each time you choose empathy over judgment, or kindness over irritation, you make the world just a little softer.

Emotional Intelligence: Your Secret Puberty Superpower

If someone told you that puberty could give you superpowers, you might laugh. But the truth is, one of the greatest powers you'll ever have starts developing right now — your *emotional intelligence.*

Emotional intelligence is the ability to recognize your feelings, understand why they're happening, and respond in a healthy way. It's also the skill of noticing how other people feel and treating them with care. It's not about hiding your emotions or pretending to be strong all the time — it's about learning how to use your emotions *wisely.*

Think about your favorite superheroes. What makes them powerful isn't just their strength — it's how they handle it. They know when to act, when to pause, and when to use their powers for good. That's exactly what emotional intelligence does for you. It helps you know when to speak up, when to take a breath, and when to walk away.

Let's say you're in a heated argument with a friend. You can feel anger bubbling up inside you, and you're tempted to say something hurtful. But then you remember that feelings don't have to control your actions. You take a breath, think about what's really bothering you, and say calmly, "I'm hurt that you didn't

Include me." That's emotional intelligence in action. You used your feelings as information, not weapons.

The more you practice this kind of awareness, the stronger it gets. Over time, you'll notice that you don't react as quickly when you're upset. You start to pause and ask yourself, *"What's the best thing to do right now?"* That pause — that moment of clarity — is your superpower.

Emotional intelligence also helps you handle disappointment, stress, and change. It teaches you how to bounce back from bad days instead of letting them define you. When you understand your emotions, they stop feeling like waves crashing over you and start feeling like tides you can learn to ride.

And here's the best part: emotional intelligence makes you shine from the inside out. People are naturally drawn to those who are calm, understanding, and kind. You'll find that as you grow in emotional strength, you'll become someone others trust — someone who brings peace instead of drama.

But remember, even superheroes have off days. You don't have to be emotionally perfect. You just have to keep learning, keep breathing, and keep showing up for yourself.

Every emotion you feel — even the uncomfortable ones — has something valuable to teach you. Sadness teaches compassion. Anger teaches courage. Joy teaches gratitude. Fear teaches awareness. Together, they shape you into someone wise, caring, and strong.

Puberty may feel like a whirlwind of changes, but it's also the season when you begin discovering your inner strength — the kind that doesn't come from pretending to be okay, but from truly *understanding* yourself.

So the next time your feelings feel big or confusing, take a breath. Listen. There's wisdom in every emotion. And within that wisdom lies the most powerful version of you — the one who feels deeply, learns bravely, and grows beautifully.

<u>Chapter 3</u>

Building Confidence and

Self-Esteem

The Confidence Equation

When Sofia looked in the mirror before school one morning, she frowned. Her hair wouldn't cooperate, her uniform felt awkward, and no matter how many times she adjusted it, something still seemed off. As she sighed, she caught her little sister watching from the doorway.

"You look so pretty," her sister said simply.

Sofia blinked. "Really?"

Her sister nodded, smiling like it was the most obvious thing in the world.

In that moment, Sofia realized something important: how we *see* ourselves isn't always how others see us. Sometimes, our minds whisper things that aren't true — small lies that chip away at how we feel about ourselves. Confidence isn't about being perfect. It's about learning to *see yourself clearly* — the way people who love you already do.

That's what self-esteem is all about.

What Self-Esteem Really Means

You've probably heard people talk about self-esteem, but what does it actually mean? It's not about thinking you're better than everyone else or pretending you're always happy. Self-esteem means *knowing your worth*, even on the days when you don't feel your best. It's about trusting that you are enough — just as you are — and believing that you deserve kindness, respect, and love, from yourself and from others.

When your self-esteem is healthy, it's like having an invisible armor around you. It doesn't mean bad things never happen, but it means they don't break you as easily. Someone might say something hurtful, but you'll be able to think, *That's their opinion — not my truth.* You'll make mistakes, but instead of giving up, you'll remind yourself, *I can learn from this.*

The truth is, confidence isn't something you're born with. It's something you build — brick by brick, moment by moment. Every time you speak kindly to yourself, every time you try something new, and every time you get back up after a bad day, you're building your self-esteem.

But it's not always easy. Growing up means facing new challenges — changing bodies, shifting friendships, school stress, and social media that can make you doubt yourself. Sometimes it feels like everyone else has it figured out, while you're stuck comparing yourself to photos, grades, or how many likes your post got.

That's where real confidence comes in. It's quiet, steady, and rooted deep inside you. It's not about how many followers you have or whether your hair looks good today. It's about *how you treat yourself when no one's watching*.

True self-esteem starts when you stop measuring your worth by outside things and start valuing who you are inside — your kindness, your creativity, your courage, your humor. Those are the things that make you unforgettable, and they don't disappear just because you have an off day.

How to Notice Negative Thoughts and Challenge Them

Have you ever caught yourself thinking things like, *I'm not good enough,* or *I'll probably mess this up anyway?* Those thoughts are sneaky. They sound convincing because they use your own voice. But they're not the truth — they're just *thoughts*.

Everyone has an inner critic — that tiny voice that loves to point out flaws or replay embarrassing moments. During puberty, that voice sometimes gets louder because your brain is more aware of how others see you.

But here's the secret: you get to decide whether you believe that voice or not.

The first step is to notice it. When a negative thought shows up, pause for a moment and ask yourself, *Would I ever say this to a friend?* Usually, the answer is no. So why say it to yourself?

Let's say you're about to give a presentation in class, and your inner critic whispers, *You're going to mess up.* Instead of accepting that thought, try talking back. *Actually, I've practiced this. I might be nervous, but I'm prepared.* It may feel strange at first, but over time, you'll start believing the kinder voice more than the mean one.

Challenging negative thoughts doesn't mean pretending you're perfect — it means giving yourself the same compassion you'd give anyone else. When you catch yourself thinking, *I look weird in this outfit,* you can counter it with, *My body is changing, and that's okay. I'm growing.* When you think, *I'm so bad at math,* remind yourself, *I'm still learning, and I can get better.*

You can even picture your negative thoughts as little clouds drifting across the sky. You don't have to chase them or argue with them — just notice them, and let them pass. The sun (your true self) is still shining behind them, even when you can't see it.

The more you practice challenging those thoughts, the quieter they become. And in their place, confidence starts to grow. Not the loud kind that needs to show off — but the calm kind that comes from knowing you can handle whatever comes your way.

Daily Confidence-Building Habits

Confidence grows through small, daily choices. It's not something you get all at once — it's something you *practice*, like a muscle that gets stronger every time you use it.

One of the simplest ways to start is through how you talk to yourself each day. Every morning, you have a chance to set the tone for how you'll treat yourself. Instead of rushing straight to your phone or worrying about what could go wrong, take a deep breath and say something kind — even something small, like *I'm ready for today* or *I can handle what comes my way.*

You can also build confidence by trying things that challenge you, even when they feel uncomfortable. It might be raising your hand in class, joining a new club, or speaking up when you have an idea. Each time you do something brave — no matter how small — you teach your brain that you're capable.

Another powerful habit is gratitude. At the end of the day, think about three things you appreciate about yourself or your day. Maybe you helped a friend, learned something new, or made someone laugh. Gratitude helps your brain focus on what's *right* instead of what's missing.

And don't forget — your body and mind are connected. Getting enough sleep, eating well, and moving your body aren't just about health; they're about confidence too. When you take care of yourself physically, your energy, focus, and mood all improve. You feel stronger, clearer, more you.

Confidence also grows when you surround yourself with the right people — friends who lift you up instead of bringing you down. Pay attention to how you feel after spending time with someone. Do you feel happy and supported, or drained and small? The people who make you feel seen and accepted are the ones who help your confidence bloom.

Most importantly, remember that confidence isn't about always feeling great. Even the most self-assured people have moments of doubt. What matters is that you keep showing up for yourself anyway. Every time you choose self-kindness over self-criticism, every time you take a deep breath instead of giving up, you're proving to yourself that you're strong.

You won't always get it right, and that's okay. Confidence isn't about perfection — it's about progress. It's about learning to see yourself not as a project that needs fixing, but as a person who's already enough, even while growing.

Confidence isn't something you wait to feel before you act — it's something you build *by* acting. Every moment you choose to believe in yourself a little more, you lay another brick in the foundation of your self-esteem.

So the next time you stand in front of the mirror, instead of searching for what's wrong, look for what's right. See the courage in your eyes. The kindness in your smile. The determination in your heart.

That's where confidence begins — not in what the world says about you, but in what *you* decide to believe about yourself.

You Are Enough

When Ava scrolled through her social media feed, it sometimes felt like everyone else's life looked perfect. Her classmates posted pictures of vacations, new clothes, flawless smiles, and perfect skin. She couldn't help but notice what she *didn't* have. Her hair didn't shine like that. Her selfies never looked as good. And sometimes, even though she had friends and good grades, she still felt like she wasn't *enough*.

Sound familiar?

You're not alone. Every girl — no matter how confident she looks on the outside — has moments when she compares herself to others and feels like she falls short. But here's the truth that many people forget to say out loud: *what you see online isn't the whole story.* It's just a highlight reel — tiny snapshots of someone's best moments. Nobody posts pictures of the times they feel sad, scared, or unsure. Everyone struggles sometimes; they just don't always show it.

And even though it's hard to remember, you don't need to be perfect to be valuable. You don't need filters or followers to be enough. You already *are.*

Overcoming Comparison and Social Media Pressure

It's easy to get caught in the trap of comparison — especially during puberty, when everything about you is changing and you're still figuring out who you are. You might compare your looks, your body, your clothes, or even your personality to others. You might think, *She's prettier,* or *He's more popular,* or *They seem so confident.* But comparison always steals your joy, because it makes you forget what's amazing about *you.*

The truth is, no one wins in the comparison game. There will always be someone taller, someone funnier, someone with trendier clothes or more followers. But none of those things make them better. They're just *different.*

When you spend your energy trying to be like everyone else, you lose the chance to be fully yourself — and that's the part of you the world actually needs. Your smile, your creativity, your kindness, your sense of humor — those are the things that make you unforgettable.

Social media can make it hard to see that clearly. The photos you see online often have filters, perfect lighting, and dozens of retakes behind them. What you're comparing yourself to isn't reality — it's a carefully edited version of someone's life. Even influencers and celebrities feel insecure sometimes.

So instead of asking, *"Why don't I look like her?"* try asking, *"What do I love about being me?"*

Maybe you love that your laugh is loud and contagious. Maybe you love how good you are at listening to others, or how creative you get when you draw, write, or dance. The things that make you different are the things that make you *shine*.

Remember: confidence isn't about being the prettiest or the most popular. It's about knowing your worth — and refusing to let comparison make you forget it.

Embracing Your Individuality and Talents

Every person in the world is one of a kind. Think about that for a moment — out of billions of people, there's no one who laughs exactly like you, dreams exactly like you, or has your exact mix of quirks, talents, and strengths. You're an original — a once-in-a-lifetime combination of everything beautiful and brave.

But it can be easy to forget that when you're surrounded by voices telling you how to act, what to wear, or what to look like. You might start to think you need to fit into a certain box to be accepted — to be quiet instead of bold, trendy instead of true to yourself. But fitting in and *belonging* aren't the same thing. Fitting in means changing yourself to be liked. Belonging means being loved for who you already are.

You don't need to shrink your personality to make other people comfortable. You don't need to hide your talents because they're "different." Your individuality is your power.

Maybe you love math or reading when others love sports. Maybe you're artistic or shy or adventurous or a mix of all three. Whatever you are, that's what makes you special. The world needs all kinds of people — thinkers, dreamers, doers, helpers, artists, leaders, and quiet observers.

Start noticing what lights you up inside. When you lose track of time because you're doing something you love — drawing, writing stories, baking, running, building something — that's a clue to who you really are. Those passions are like little sparks that show you your path.

You don't need to compare your spark to anyone else's. A candle doesn't compete with the sun — both have their purpose, and both give light in their own way. Your job isn't to be like someone else's glow; it's to keep your own shining bright.

The Art of Speaking Kindly to Yourself

The words you say to yourself matter more than any words someone else could say to you. Your thoughts become the voice you hear most often — and they can either build you up or tear you down. That's why learning to speak kindly to yourself is one of the most powerful things you can ever do.

If you've ever looked in the mirror and said, *"I hate my nose,"* or *"I'm so awkward,"* you already know how harsh that voice can be. But imagine if your best friend said those things about herself. You'd rush to tell her, *"That's not true! You're amazing!"* You deserve to speak to yourself with that same care.

Speaking kindly to yourself doesn't mean pretending you're perfect. It means being gentle with yourself when you make mistakes. It means saying, *"I can try again,"* instead of, *"I always mess up."* It means noticing your strengths instead of focusing only on your flaws.

Your body hears everything your mind says. When you talk to yourself with love — saying, *"I'm learning,"* *"I'm proud of myself,"* or *"I am enough"* — your brain actually starts to believe it. Over time, those kind thoughts grow stronger, and the negative ones get quieter.

One beautiful way to practice this is by creating a few "power phrases" that remind you of your worth. You can write them on sticky notes and put them on your mirror, your notebook, or your phone case. Every time you see them, take a breath and repeat them in your mind.

Try simple ones like:
"I am growing and learning every day."
"My uniqueness is my strength."
"I am enough — just as I am."

Saying these words isn't silly or self-centered — it's self-respect. You're training your heart to believe what's already true: that you are worthy of kindness, love, and confidence right now — not someday, not when you've changed, but now.

When you start speaking kindly to yourself, you'll notice something amazing: the way you see the world starts to change too. You'll find it easier to be kind to others, to celebrate their successes without comparing them to your own. You'll realize that kindness — to yourself and to others — always multiplies.

Growing up in today's world can feel like standing in front of a million mirrors, each reflecting a slightly different version of who you could be. But the only reflection that truly matters is the one that comes from within — the one that says, *I'm doing my best, I'm learning, and that's enough.*

There's nothing you need to prove to be worthy. You don't have to earn love, beauty, or belonging. You already have them inside you.

So the next time you find yourself scrolling through perfect pictures or doubting your own sparkle, remember this: nobody else can be you. And that's your greatest gift.

You are not behind. You are not too much or not enough.
You are exactly who you're meant to be — growing, learning, and becoming someone incredible.

You are, and always have been, *enough.*

Shine Bright

There's a moment that happens to every girl — a quiet shift when she begins to notice her own light. It doesn't come with applause or fireworks. Sometimes it happens on an ordinary day — maybe after helping a friend, finishing a drawing you're proud of, or standing up for yourself when it wasn't easy. You feel it deep inside, a little spark that says, *"I did that."*

That spark? That's confidence growing. And learning how to nurture it — especially during puberty, when so many things are changing — is one of the greatest gifts you can give yourself.

Your light isn't something you have to earn or compete for. It's already inside you. You just need to learn how to see it, care for it, and let it shine.

Using Gratitude and Self-Affirmations

When life feels messy or confusing, gratitude can be your gentle anchor. It's not about pretending everything is perfect — it's about finding small pockets of good, even on tough days. Gratitude shifts your focus from what's missing to what's already here.

Think of it like this: your mind is like a flashlight. Wherever you point it, that's what lights up. If you always point it toward worries, insecurities, or things that frustrate you, your world will feel dim. But when you aim it toward moments of gratitude — even tiny ones — everything starts to glow a little brighter.

You can start with something as simple as, *"I'm thankful for my cozy bed,"* or *"I'm grateful that my best friend made me laugh today."* The more you notice the good things, the more they seem to multiply. Gratitude is like watering a plant — what you nourish grows.

Self-affirmations work the same way, but instead of noticing the good *around* you, they help you see the good *within* you. An affirmation is a sentence that reminds your heart of its truth — something strong, kind, and powerful about who you are.

You might say:
"I am learning and growing every day."
"I am kind, brave, and enough."
"I can handle hard things."

At first, saying these things might feel awkward — especially if you don't fully believe them yet. But that's exactly why they matter. Your brain listens to what you repeat. Over time, those words begin to shape how you see yourself. The same way you wouldn't expect to get strong after one push-up, you can't expect confidence to grow overnight. But with daily practice, it does.

Try saying your affirmations while looking in the mirror, or whispering them before you go to sleep. The more you speak kindly to yourself, the more that kindness becomes your default voice — the one that gently drowns out the inner critic that says, *"I'm not good enough."*

Gratitude and affirmations are like twin habits of happiness. One helps you see what's good around you; the other helps you see what's good within you. Together, they help your confidence bloom naturally.

Celebrating Small Wins During Puberty

Puberty can sometimes feel like a roller coaster you didn't sign up for — full of ups, downs, and loops you didn't expect. Some days you feel proud of your growth, and other days you might wish things would just slow down. But here's a secret that confident people know: growth doesn't always look glamorous. It's made of small wins — quiet victories that show how far you've come, even if no one else notices.

Think about the first time you handled a difficult emotion without snapping at someone. Or the moment you walked into school feeling nervous but still held your head high. Maybe you finally talked to someone you were too shy to approach before, or got through a bad day without letting it define you. Those are wins worth celebrating.

You don't need a trophy or a big announcement. Sometimes, the best celebrations are the ones you keep in your heart — the ones that remind you that you're becoming stronger, wiser, and more comfortable being yourself.

Celebrating small wins trains your brain to see progress instead of perfection. Instead of thinking, *"I'm not there yet,"* you start thinking, *"Look how far I've already come."* And that shift — from frustration to appreciation — builds lasting confidence.

You can even create a "confidence journal" or a "victory jar" where you jot down your small achievements. They don't have to be huge — maybe you spoke up in class, tried something new, or took care of yourself when you felt down. Every few weeks, look back at what you've written. You'll be amazed by how many moments of courage you've already had.

Puberty is full of milestones — physical, emotional, and social. You'll notice new things about your body, learn how to handle bigger feelings, and discover more about your personality. Each step, no matter how tiny, is part of your transformation. So give yourself credit for every bit of growth. You deserve it.

Creating Your Personal "Confidence Mantra"

Confidence isn't something you find once and keep forever — it's something you practice, like a favorite song you return to when you need strength. That's where your **confidence mantra** comes in.

A mantra is a short, powerful phrase that helps you center yourself when life feels overwhelming. It's like a compass that points you back to your worth, no matter what's happening around you.

Your confidence mantra should feel like a warm hug from your future self — strong, loving, and full of belief. It could be something like:

"I am becoming the best version of myself."
"I don't have to be perfect to be proud."
"I am brave, even when I'm scared."
"My voice matters."

When you repeat your mantra, you're reminding your mind to stay calm, grounded, and kind. You can say it in your head before a test, while walking into a new class, or whenever you start to doubt yourself. Over time, it becomes like a secret source of strength — a quiet reminder that you've got this.

Some girls like to write their mantra on sticky notes and put them on their mirror. Others keep it in their journal or wear a bracelet engraved with a special word. However you carry it, what matters most is that it feels *real* to you — something that makes your heart lift a little when you say it.

Your mantra doesn't have to stay the same forever. You might change it as you grow and learn more about yourself. What's constant is the message behind it: *You are strong, capable, and worthy — exactly as you are.*

Confidence doesn't happen because everything in your life is perfect. It happens when you learn how to see yourself through kind eyes — to notice your progress, speak your truth, and keep shining even when the world feels unsure.

Some days your light might feel small, like a flicker. Other days, it will burn bright enough to light up the room. Both are okay. What matters is that you keep tending to it — with gratitude, affirmations, small celebrations, and words that lift you higher.

You don't need anyone's permission to shine. You don't need to be flawless or fearless. All you need to do is show up as yourself — again and again — and trust that your light is enough.

Because it is.

It always has been.

E.J. Rico

So keep shining, bright girl. The world needs your glow.

Chapter 4

Friendship Upgrades —

Navigating Changes in Your

Relationships

When Friendships Change

Mia and Ella had been best friends since kindergarten. They did everything together — shared snacks, swapped secrets, and even had matching bracelets that said "Besties Forever." But by the time they reached middle school, something felt different. Ella started spending more time with a new group of friends who loved makeup and pop bands, while Mia still preferred sketching in her notebook and reading during lunch. One day, Mia overheard Ella laughing with someone else about how she'd "changed."

That night, Mia lay in bed wondering what went wrong. She missed her friend but didn't know how to talk about it. She wondered if she'd done something wrong, or if this was just what growing up felt like.

If you've ever felt that ache — when a friendship that once felt unbreakable suddenly feels fragile — you're not alone. Puberty doesn't just change your body and emotions; it changes your relationships, too. And while it can be confusing or even painful, it's also a natural part of growing up.

Friendships shift during puberty for many reasons. As you and your friends grow, your interests, personalities, and even values might start to change. You might want different things, hang out with new people, or explore new sides of yourself. Sometimes these changes bring friends closer together, and sometimes they create distance. It's not always because of a fight or betrayal — often, it's simply because you're both evolving.

And that's okay.

When you were younger, friendships were often built around playtime, shared toys, or favorite shows. But as you grow, friendships start to depend more on emotional connection — people who understand you, listen to you, and support you for who you are. It's normal for some friendships to drift apart as others grow deeper.

That doesn't mean the memories stop mattering. It just means the friendship had its special time and purpose in your story. Letting go doesn't erase what was real. It simply makes room for what's next.

Why Friendships Sometimes Drift or Shift During Puberty

During puberty, you begin discovering new parts of yourself. You might become more independent, start forming stronger opinions, or notice that you and your friends see the world differently. Maybe you love science, but your friend loves fashion. Maybe you want to talk about books, and she wants to talk about crushes.

These differences don't mean your friendship is over — but they might mean it needs to change.

Sometimes, friends drift apart because of new interests, but sometimes it's about emotions. As your feelings get stronger and your social world expands, misunderstandings can happen more easily. Maybe a friend doesn't text you back right away, and you take it personally. Or maybe someone you used to tell everything to suddenly seems distant.

When that happens, it's important to remember that both of you are figuring things out. Puberty can make people moody or distracted without meaning to hurt anyone. It's not always about you — sometimes, your friend is just dealing with her own changes.

If you start to feel left out or confused, try to talk about it honestly. You might say, "I feel like we don't hang out as much. Is everything okay between us?" Sometimes, one conversation can clear up a misunderstanding and bring you closer again. But even if it doesn't, know this: friendships aren't meant to stay the same forever. Some grow with you, and others gently fade. Both can still be beautiful.

How to Handle Jealousy, Gossip, or Misunderstandings

Friendships during puberty can sometimes feel like emotional puzzles — full of loyalty, confusion, and unexpected challenges. Jealousy might creep in when a friend spends more time with someone else. Gossip might spread and hurt feelings. Misunderstandings can make even kind girls feel defensive or distant.

Jealousy is one of those feelings that no one likes to admit, but everyone feels at some point. It doesn't make you a bad friend — it makes you human. It usually shows up when you care deeply about someone and fear losing your place in their life. The key is to notice that feeling without letting it control you. Instead of thinking, *"She likes her more than me,"* try asking yourself, *"Why do I feel left out, and what do I need right now?"* Sometimes, it's reassurance. Sometimes, it's a reminder that you can have more than one important friendship in your life.

Gossip, on the other hand, can feel tempting — especially when it helps you feel included in a group. But gossip always costs something. It can hurt trust, break bonds, and make people afraid to open up. If you find yourself in a situation where friends are talking about someone, pause for a second. Ask yourself if you'd feel okay if the same words were about you. If not, you have the power to change the topic or quietly walk away. That simple act shows true strength — the kind that earns respect.

And then there are misunderstandings — those awkward moments when something small spirals into something big. Maybe a friend didn't invite you somewhere, or someone said something that sounded rude but wasn't meant that way. When that happens, try to take a breath before reacting. Emotions run high during puberty, and sometimes, what you assume isn't the full story.

Talking things out — calmly and kindly — can fix more than you think. You might start with, *"I just want to understand what happened,"* or *"It hurt my feelings when..."* Those conversations aren't easy, but they show maturity and self-respect. Not every friendship will last forever, but honest communication gives it a better chance to grow stronger.

Knowing When to Let Go Gracefully

One of the hardest lessons about friendship is learning when to hold on — and when to let go. Sometimes, no matter how kind or loyal you are, a friendship starts to feel one-sided, uncomfortable, or even hurtful. Maybe your friend makes fun of you, ignores your feelings, or only talks to you when it's convenient. It's painful, especially when you remember how close you once were.

But letting go doesn't mean you stop caring. It means you start caring for yourself.

Healthy friendships should make you feel supported, not small. They should bring peace, not constant drama. If you're always walking on eggshells or trying to prove your worth, it might be time to take a step back. You don't have to make a big announcement or end things with anger. Sometimes, distance happens naturally — fewer texts, less time together — and that's okay.

Think of friendships like seasons. Some last for years, growing deeper with time. Others come and go, teaching you something important before fading. Each friendship — even the ones that end — shapes you in some way. Maybe it taught you how to set boundaries, how to listen better, or how to stand up for yourself. That growth is never wasted.

If a friendship ends, allow yourself to feel sad. It's okay to miss someone who once meant a lot to you. But also remember: endings create space for new beginnings. You'll meet people who match your energy, who laugh at your jokes, and who love you exactly as you are.

Letting go gracefully is about gratitude — being thankful for the moments you shared, even as you release what no longer fits. It's about trusting that your circle will change, but your worth never will.

Friendship during puberty is a journey — full of surprises, challenges, and beautiful lessons. Some friends will walk beside you for years; others will join you for a little while. But every experience helps you understand who you are and what kind of friend you want to be.

So when friendships change, don't see it as losing something. See it as *becoming* something — wiser, kinder, and more in tune with the kind of love and connection you deserve.

Because every time you choose kindness over jealousy, honesty over gossip, and self-respect over trying too hard — you're building the kind of confidence that makes every friendship stronger.

How to Be a Good Friend

The first time Leila realized she hadn't really *listened* to her best friend, she was surprised. Her friend Maya had been talking about something that upset her — how left out she felt during group projects — but Leila had been half-focused, scrolling through her phone and saying "uh-huh" without really hearing. When Maya suddenly went quiet, Leila looked up and saw tears in her friend's eyes.

"I just needed someone to listen," Maya said softly.

That moment stayed with Leila. It made her realize something powerful — being a good friend isn't just about laughing together or having sleepovers. It's about showing up with your whole heart — listening, caring, and being honest even when it's not easy.

Friendship, especially during puberty, is like a dance. Sometimes it feels effortless, and other times you step on each other's toes. But the secret to keeping friendships strong isn't perfection. It's *presence*. It's choosing to be the kind of friend who listens deeply, sets healthy boundaries, and builds trust — one kind act at a time.

Listening with Your Heart

Listening might sound simple, but real listening — the kind that makes someone feel seen and safe — is rare and beautiful. It means paying attention not just to someone's words but to their feelings, their body language, and what they *don't* say.

When your friend tells you she's had a bad day, listening isn't about jumping in to fix it or changing the topic to your own story. It's about being there — quiet, patient, and caring. Sometimes, all someone needs is to know they're not alone.

During puberty, emotions can feel louder — and not just yours. Your friends might be going through changes too: feeling insecure, jealous, or anxious without knowing why. Being a good listener helps them feel understood. It's like saying, *"I see you, and your feelings matter."*

Listening doesn't mean agreeing with everything or staying silent when something feels wrong. It means giving your friend space to express themselves before you respond. When you truly listen, you create trust — the kind that makes people feel safe opening up to you again.

It's okay if you're still learning how. No one gets it perfect all the time. What matters most is your I ntention — showing your friend that you care enough to stop, look, and really hear them. That's where real connection begins.

Honesty and Empathy: The Heart of True Friendship

Good friends tell the truth — not to hurt, but to help. Honesty is the foundation of every strong friendship because it builds trust. But it's not just *what* you say that matters — it's *how* you say it.

There's a big difference between saying, *"That outfit looks weird,"* and saying, *"I think the other one brings out your eyes more."* Honesty mixed with kindness becomes empathy — the ability to care about how your words affect someone else.

Empathy is like emotional super-vision. It helps you step into someone else's shoes and imagine how they might feel. Maybe your friend didn't text you back because she's overwhelmed, not because she's ignoring you. Maybe she's quiet because she's worried, not because she's mad. When you learn to look beyond your own feelings and consider hers too, you become the kind of friend everyone wants — compassionate and understanding.

Puberty can make empathy even more important. Everyone's confidence is shifting, emotions are stronger, and misunderstandings can spread fast. Being honest and empathetic helps keep friendships grounded through all the changes.

That doesn't mean you have to be perfect or always say the right thing. Sometimes you'll say something you regret. When that happens, the best thing you can do is own it. A simple, *"I'm sorry I hurt your feelings — I didn't mean to,"* can repair more than you realize. It shows maturity, humility, and care — all signs of a truly good friend.

The most powerful friendships are built not on pretending everything is fine, but on telling the truth with love — and forgiving when others do the same.

How to Set Healthy Boundaries Kindly

One of the hardest but most important parts of being a good friend is learning to set boundaries — knowing when to say yes, when to say no, and when to take space for yourself.

It might sound scary. You might worry that setting boundaries will make people think you're mean or selfish. But the truth is, boundaries don't push people away — they help relationships grow in a healthy way.

Imagine you're a glass of water. Every time you listen, help, or give your energy to someone, a little water pours out. But if you never refill your glass — if you keep giving without resting — you eventually run dry. Boundaries are how you refill your glass.

Sometimes that means saying, *"I can't talk right now, but I care about you,"* or *"I need some space today."* It might mean deciding not to be around people who gossip or pressure you into things that don't feel right.

A good friend respects your limits because she knows your "no" isn't rejection — it's self-care. And you should respect hers, too.

Setting boundaries kindly also means understanding that not every friendship will be perfect all the time. You might have different opinions or need breaks from each other. That's normal. What matters is how you handle it — with respect, not resentment.

Healthy boundaries actually make friendships stronger because they're built on honesty and understanding instead of guilt or obligation. You don't have to give everything to be loved. You just have to be genuine, and that's enough.

Building Trust and Respect

Trust is like a mirror — once broken, it takes time to repair. That's why building and keeping trust is one of the most precious parts of friendship. It's about keeping secrets safe, telling the truth even when it's hard, and showing up when your friend needs you most.

When someone confides in you, it's not just words — it's a gift. They're saying, *"I trust you with this piece of me."* Protect it. Don't share it, even if you think it's harmless. Once trust is broken, it can take a long time to rebuild.

Respect goes hand in hand with trust. It means accepting your friend for who she is — even when she's different from you. Maybe she's more outgoing or more quiet, more emotional or more logical. You don't have to understand every part of her to care about her. Respect means loving your friends for their uniqueness — and expecting the same in return.

Building trust also means showing up — not just when it's fun, but when it's hard. It means being honest when your friend asks for advice, and gentle when she's struggling. It's remembering birthdays, cheering for her successes, and being the shoulder she can cry on when things don't go right.

And just as important — it means trusting *yourself.* Trust that you're worthy of good friendships. Trust that the people who truly care about you will stay. And trust that even when friendships change, you'll always have the tools to build new ones — stronger, kinder, and truer each time.

Being a good friend doesn't mean being perfect. It means trying — every day — to show up with honesty, empathy, and kindness. It's listening when someone needs to talk. It's apologizing when you hurt someone. It's standing by people when life feels messy and celebrating them when things go well.

Friendship during puberty can feel complicated, but it's also one of the most beautiful parts of growing up. You're learning how to love and be loved in ways that shape who you'll become.

Every time you choose kindness over gossip, empathy over judgment, and boundaries over burnout — you're not just being a good friend. You're being a good *you*.

And that kind of friendship — the one that starts within yourself — is the kind that lasts forever.

The Friendship Circle

When you think about your closest friends — the ones who make you laugh so hard your stomach hurts or who just *get* you without needing to explain — those are your "real ones." The ones who make life brighter simply by being part of it.

But during puberty, figuring out who those real friends are can be tricky. People change. Groups shift. Someone you thought would always be there might start hanging out with new people. Sometimes, friendships get tested by jealousy, rumors, or misunderstandings.

Still, this is also the time when some of the most meaningful friendships of your life can begin — the kind that don't just fill your days but help shape who you're becoming.

Finding your *friendship circle* isn't about having the most friends or being part of the "right group." It's about finding the people who see you, appreciate you, and bring out your best self.

Finding Your "Real Ones" — Friends Who Uplift You

Real friends are like sunshine on cloudy days — they make things lighter just by showing up. You know them not because they're perfect, but because they make you feel comfortable being *you*.

You don't have to pretend with them. You don't have to shrink or exaggerate. They cheer for your wins and stay when you're struggling. They tell you the truth kindly, listen when you need to vent, and never make you feel small for feeling big things.

But sometimes, before you find your "real ones," you'll meet people who make you doubt yourself — friends who make you feel like you have to work to be accepted. That's not what real friendship feels like. It shouldn't make you anxious or exhausted.

Friendships that uplift you will always have space for laughter, honesty, and growth. You'll know it's right when being around someone feels easy, even in silence.

And here's a secret — finding true friends starts with *being* one. When you're kind, trustworthy, and genuine, you attract people with the same energy. The universe has a funny way of bringing like-hearted people together.

Don't worry if your circle feels small right now. It's not about the number of friends you have; it's about how those friendships make you feel. Sometimes, one loyal, kind, and honest friend is worth more than a hundred people who only show up when it's convenient.

Standing Up for Others

Being a good friend isn't just about the moments when everything is easy — it's about how you act when it's not. Standing up for someone, especially when they're being teased or left out, takes real courage. But that kind of courage is what makes friendships strong and communities kinder.

You've probably seen it happen before — a classmate getting whispered about or laughed at, and everyone pretending not to notice. It's uncomfortable. Your heart races because you *know* it's wrong, but you don't want to stand out or become the next target.

Here's what most people don't realize: when you stay silent, you give the unkindness power. But when you speak up — even in small ways — you remind everyone what kindness looks like.

You don't have to make a big scene. Sometimes it's as simple as saying, "That's not funny," or quietly standing next to the person who's being left out. Other times, it might mean reaching out later and saying, "Hey, are you okay? Want to sit with me?"

Those small acts make a huge difference. They show others that compassion is stronger than cruelty. And when you stand up for someone, you also teach your circle what real friendship means — loyalty, empathy, and courage.

You might be surprised how many people will admire you for it — even if they don't say it out loud. True confidence doesn't come from popularity or likes on social media; it comes from doing what's right, even when it's hard.

The world needs more girls who lift others up instead of tearing them down. And the beautiful thing is — that power is already inside you. Every time you choose kindness, you make your circle, your school, and your world a little better.

Activities That Strengthen Friendships

Friendships grow stronger not just through deep talks, but through shared memories — the small, fun, spontaneous things you do together that make you both laugh until you can't breathe. These moments build connection and trust without needing big plans or grand gestures.

It might be as simple as walking home together and talking about your favorite songs, or having "no phone days" where you just hang out and bake cookies, draw, or watch old movies. When you do things that make you both happy, you create a rhythm — something special that keeps you connected even when life gets busier.

Friendship also deepens when you support each other's passions. Maybe your friend loves sports, and you go cheer her on. Maybe you're into art, and she helps you hang your drawings for a school exhibit. When you show genuine interest in what matters to each other, your friendship becomes a safe space for growth.

Even when disagreements happen — and they will — those shared experiences remind you that your friendship is worth working through. Laughter, patience, and forgiveness are like the glue that holds your friendship circle together.

You can also strengthen friendships through kindness projects — volunteering together, starting a "positivity wall" at school, or writing encouraging notes to classmates. Doing good *together* brings a deeper sense of purpose and connection.

And don't forget, friendship isn't always about doing; sometimes it's about *being*. Being present. Being understanding. Being that person who says, *"I'm here,"* even when you don't have all the answers.

The more you grow, the more you'll realize that your friendship circle is one of the most powerful forces in your life. It can shape your confidence, influence your choices, and color your memories. So choose carefully — and kindly.

Choose the friends who bring out your best laugh. The ones who listen when you're quiet. The ones who remind you of your worth when you forget it yourself.

And just as importantly, *be* that kind of friend for someone else.

When your circle is built on love, respect, laughter, and honesty, it becomes unbreakable — not because you never fight or disagree, but because you always find your way back to understanding.

Friendship, at its best, is a mirror that reflects your best self. And when you surround yourself with people who make you feel strong, supported, and seen — you'll shine even brighter.

Because the real magic of friendship isn't just about having people to share your secrets with. It's about having people who remind you who you are — and help you love that person more every day.

<u>Chapter 5</u>

Body Care and Self-Care Habits

(

Hygiene and Health 101

When you wake up in the morning, you might notice things that didn't use to happen before — your skin feels a little oilier, your hair gets greasy faster, or your underarms need more attention than they used to. Welcome to one of the most natural parts of growing up — learning how to take care of your changing body.

This isn't about trying to be perfect or looking like someone else. It's about feeling good in your own skin, learning what your body needs, and treating it with care and respect. Puberty brings a lot of changes — some exciting, some confusing — but one thing's for sure: the more you understand what's happening, the more confident you'll feel handling it.

Body care is not just about staying clean — it's about self-love. When you take the time to care for your body, you're also saying, *"I matter. I'm worth taking care of."*

Daily Hygiene Routines and Body Changes

As your body matures, your sweat glands start working differently, and your hormones become more active. This means you might notice body odor, oilier hair, and breakouts — totally normal signs that your body is doing its job.

You might need to adjust some of your daily routines. Showering regularly, especially after physical activity, helps keep your skin fresh and your confidence up. You'll also want to start using deodorant or antiperspirant if you notice underarm odor. It's not about hiding who you are — it's about keeping yourself comfortable and confident in your skin.

Your face might also go through changes. Some days, your skin will look clear and smooth; other days, it might feel bumpy or oily. This is because your pores can produce more oil during puberty, leading to acne. Gentle cleansing is key — nothing too harsh or drying. A mild cleanser twice a day, a clean pillowcase, and avoiding touching your face too much can make a big difference.

And yes — hair will start growing in new places, too. Under your arms, on your legs, maybe even a bit above your lip. You get to decide what to do about it. Some girls choose to shave, while others don't. There's no "right" answer — it's all about what makes *you* feel comfortable. If you do choose to shave, ask a trusted adult to show you how to do it safely.

Your body is learning to balance itself. Some days you'll feel graceful, other days a bit awkward — that's all part of the process. The important thing is to listen to your body and care for it gently.

Period Care Made Easy (Pads, Tampons, and Tracking Cycles)

One of the biggest changes that happens during puberty is getting your period — a natural sign that your body is healthy and growing. It can seem a little scary at first, especially if you don't know what to expect, but once you understand what's happening, it becomes just another part of your routine.

Your period is your body's way of shedding the lining of your uterus every month when there's no pregnancy. It's your body's rhythm — a natural cycle that connects you with every woman who's come before you.

When your period first starts, the flow is usually light, and it might take a few months to become regular. Pads are a great place to start because they're easy to use and comfortable. There are different sizes — smaller ones for lighter days, larger ones for heavier flow. Once you get used to your cycle, you might decide to try tampons or period underwear — both are safe when used properly.

Remember to change your pad or tampon regularly — about every 3–4 hours — to stay clean and avoid irritation. And if you're ever unsure, ask someone you trust — your mom, sister, aunt, or a school nurse. Every girl learns at her own pace, and there's no rush to "figure it all out" right away.

Another helpful tip? Track your cycle. You can use a journal, a calendar, or a free app. Tracking helps you predict when your next period might come and notice patterns — like when you tend to feel extra tired, moody, or hungry. That awareness helps you prepare and care for yourself better.

Cramps, bloating, or backaches can happen, too, but there are ways to ease them — gentle stretching, a warm compress, or even your favorite comfort snack can help. Most importantly, be kind to yourself during your period. Rest if you need to. Drink water. Wear comfy clothes. Your body is doing something incredible — it deserves care, not criticism.

Exercise and Nutrition for Growing Bodies

You don't have to be an athlete to move your body. Movement is one of the best ways to feel stronger, calmer, and more connected to yourself. Exercise isn't about trying to look a certain way — it's about feeling energized, releasing stress, and keeping your body healthy as it grows.

Find something you actually enjoy — dancing in your room, swimming, biking, doing yoga, or walking your dog. The best kind of exercise is the one that makes you smile while you do it. When you move regularly, your body releases endorphins — those feel-good hormones that help balance your moods, reduce stress, and even ease period cramps.

Eating well also plays a big part in feeling good. Your body is growing fast, and it needs fuel — real, colorful, nourishing foods that make you feel strong. That means mixing fruits, vegetables, whole grains, and proteins into your meals. You don't need to follow a strict "diet." Just listen to your body — eat when you're hungry, stop when you're full, and choose foods that make you feel energized instead of sluggish.

And yes, treats are part of balance, too. A piece of chocolate, a slice of pizza, or an ice cream cone with friends can all fit into a healthy lifestyle. What matters most is how you feel — inside and out.

Don't forget about hydration — your body needs water to function at its best. It helps your skin, digestion, and energy levels. Carry a water bottle to school or keep one near your desk. Think of water as your daily self-care tool — simple, free, and powerful.

Taking care of your body during puberty isn't about following rules — it's about learning to listen to yourself. Every girl's body is different. What works for your friend might not be right for you, and that's okay.

You're building a relationship with your body — one that will last your whole life. Treat it with patience, curiosity, and kindness. When you care for yourself — with hygiene, rest, movement, and love — you're not just keeping your body healthy; you're honoring the amazing girl you're becoming.

Because one day, when you look back, you'll realize something beautiful: you didn't just grow taller, stronger, or older — you grew into a girl who knew how to care for herself, inside and out.

Beauty from the Inside Out

When Ella looked in the mirror one morning, she frowned. Her hair was sticking up in five different directions, a new pimple had appeared on her chin, and she felt like her face didn't look like the girls she saw on social media. "Why can't I just look *normal*?" she muttered, tugging at her ponytail in frustration.

But later that day, something unexpected happened. Her best friend, Lily, smiled at her and said, "You always have this light in your eyes when you laugh. It's my favorite thing about you."

Ella realized something powerful — beauty isn't just about mirrors or makeup. It's about the light you bring into the world, the kindness in your words, and the way you make others feel when they're around you.

Growing up comes with all kinds of physical changes — your skin, hair, and body are constantly adjusting. But as much as it's important to care for your outside, what really makes you glow is what's happening inside: your rest, your thoughts, your heart, and how you treat yourself and others.

Sleep, Hydration, and Mindset as Part of Self-Care

There's something magical about the way your body restores itself when you rest. While you sleep, your skin repairs, your brain organizes everything you learned that day, and your mood resets for a fresh start. That's why getting enough sleep isn't just a chore — it's one of the most powerful beauty secrets there is.

When you stay up too late scrolling on your phone or binge-watching shows, your body misses that chance to recharge. You might notice dark circles, dull skin, or just feel cranky the next morning. Your body is speaking to you — asking for care.

Making sleep a priority doesn't mean you have to be perfect about it. Just find a bedtime routine that feels calm — like listening to soft music, reading, or journaling about your day. The goal is to let your body know, *"It's time to rest now."* When you treat sleep as a gift, you'll wake up with more energy, clearer skin, and a happier mind.

Hydration is another form of love your body needs daily. Water helps everything — from keeping your skin smooth to giving your brain the power to think clearly. You might not realize it, but even small habits like keeping a water bottle by your bed or bringing one to school can make a big difference.

And then there's mindset — something you can't see in the mirror but that changes how you experience everything. When you speak kindly to yourself, your body reacts. You hold your shoulders higher, your smile comes easier, and your confidence shines through naturally.

Think of your thoughts like seeds. The ones you water will grow. If you say, *"I'm so awkward"* or *"I hate my skin,"* those thoughts take root. But if you replace them with, *"I'm learning to love myself"* or *"My body is growing, and that's amazing,"* something shifts. You start seeing yourself the way the people who love you already do — with gentleness and pride.

Learning to Love Your Reflection

Loving your reflection doesn't happen overnight. Some mornings you'll wake up and feel confident, and other days you'll want to hide under your blanket. That's okay. Every girl — even the ones who seem completely sure of themselves — feels insecure sometimes.

What matters is how you talk to that girl in the mirror when those moments come.

Instead of picking out what you don't like, start noticing what makes you *you*. Maybe it's your expressive eyes, your smile, or even the way your dimples show up when you laugh. Maybe it's something you can't see — your sense of humor, your creativity, your determination.

You don't have to love everything about your appearance right away. Loving yourself is more like a friendship that deepens over time. You learn to appreciate your body for what it *does*, not just how it looks — how your legs help you run, how your arms hug the people you care about, how your heart beats strong through every adventure.

Try this: every time you look in the mirror, find one kind thing to say to yourself. It can be as simple as, *"You're trying your best today,"* or *"You have a kind heart."* The more you practice, the easier it becomes.

Because when you love your reflection — not out of vanity, but out of appreciation — you're not just building self-esteem. You're building peace.

Real Beauty = Confidence + Kindness

The world often tries to tell girls that beauty comes from the outside — from filters, makeup, or what's trending. But real beauty isn't about fitting into anyone else's definition. It's about confidence and kindness — two things that never go out of style.

Confidence isn't loud or perfect. It's quiet strength. It's the calm that comes from knowing who you are and not needing to change yourself to please others. You show confidence when you raise your hand in class, stand up for someone being teased, or wear something you love even if it's not "in."

Kindness, on the other hand, is what makes your beauty unforgettable. You can have the most flawless skin or stylish clothes, but if your heart isn't kind, none of it lasts. Kindness is what makes people remember you — the way you smile at someone who's nervous, share a seat with a new student, or compliment a classmate who's having a rough day.

When confidence and kindness come together, they create a glow that no product can match. It's the kind of beauty that inspires others to be their best selves, too.

You might notice that the people you admire most aren't necessarily the ones who look perfect, but the ones who radiate warmth, joy, and authenticity. That's the kind of beauty that never fades — the beauty that grows with you.

So the next time you catch your reflection and start to pick apart the tiny things you don't like, pause. Smile at yourself instead. Remind yourself that your beauty isn't limited to your reflection — it's in your laughter, your kindness, and your courage to keep growing.

You don't need to be flawless to shine. You just need to be real, gentle with yourself, and willing to see the beauty that's already there.

Because the truth is, every girl has her own kind of sparkle — and yours is already glowing.

Creating Your Self-Care Routine

The first time Mia tried to start a "self-care routine," she wrote out a long list: drink more water, meditate, stretch, read before bed, keep her room spotless, avoid sweets, and wake up early. It sounded perfect on paper — but by day three, she was already frustrated. "I can't do all this every day," she sighed, tossing her notebook aside.

What Mia didn't realize was that self-care isn't about perfection or sticking to a long checklist. It's about **paying attention to what your body, mind, and heart need** — and giving yourself permission to slow down and respond.

Self-care doesn't have to take hours or require fancy products. It's about small, consistent habits that help you feel grounded, calm, and confident. It's about creating moments in your day — even just a few minutes — to take care of *you*.

When you learn to care for yourself in simple, loving ways, everything else — your mood, energy, focus, and confidence — begins to shift.

Quick Morning and Evening Check-Ins

Your day begins and ends with you. Those quiet moments — before the world gets busy and just before you fall asleep — are your best chances to reconnect with yourself. Think of them as little "check-ins," where you pause, breathe, and ask: *How am I doing right now?*

In the morning, your check-in might look like standing in front of the mirror, brushing your hair, and saying, "I'm ready for today." Maybe it's writing one sentence in your journal about what you're grateful for or setting a tiny intention like, *"I'll try to be kind to myself today."*

It doesn't have to be serious or structured — even a smile at your reflection counts. That small act tells your mind, *I'm worth showing up for.*

Evening check-ins are just as important. After a long day of school, activities, and emotions, your body and brain need time to unwind. Maybe you dim the lights, change into comfy clothes, and write a few lines about your day. You could note one good thing that happened, one thing you learned, or one thing you're proud of — even if it's something small, like *"I handled a tough moment without snapping."*

These moments are powerful because they remind you that your feelings matter and that every day is part of your growth. The more you practice tuning in to yourself, the better you'll understand what helps you feel your best — and that's the heart of self-care.

Making Self-Care Fun, Not a Chore

If self-care starts to feel like another thing on your to-do list, it's easy to lose motivation. That's why it's important to make it something you *look forward to*, not something you "have to do."

Think of self-care as your personal happiness project — an ongoing adventure in finding what makes you feel relaxed, strong, and alive. Maybe that means listening to your favorite songs while getting ready, lighting a candle that smells like vanilla, or taking an extra five minutes to dance around your room before bed.

Some girls find self-care in movement — stretching, walking, or doing yoga with calming music. Others find it in creativity — drawing, journaling, decorating their space, or baking something delicious. What matters is that it feels like *you*.

Self-care can also be about laughter. Spend time with friends who make you smile. Watch a funny video. Make goofy faces in the mirror. Joy is healing, too.

You don't need expensive skincare or a complicated morning routine to take care of yourself. True self-care is choosing what nourishes your body and heart — and letting go of what doesn't.

If a "perfect" morning routine online makes you feel guilty instead of inspired, skip it. Your version of self-care doesn't have to look like anyone else's. It might be a quiet breakfast by the window, or ten minutes of journaling before school, or simply remembering to take deep breaths during stressful moments.

You're not doing self-care *wrong* if it looks simple. Sometimes, the kindest thing you can do for yourself is to take a deep breath, unclench your shoulders, and whisper, *I'm proud of myself today.*

Printable Checklist or Journal Habit Tracker Suggestion

Imagine opening a journal that feels like your safe space — filled with doodles, thoughts, and small reminders of how far you've come. A self-care tracker can be part of that — not to pressure you, but to help you celebrate progress.

You can draw a simple chart or use stickers, colors, or symbols. Maybe each day you check off things like *drank water, took three deep breaths, said something kind to myself,* or *wrote in my journal.* Over time, you'll notice patterns — what helps your mood, what drains your energy, and what makes you feel proud.

You can also add affirmations or quotes you love on the pages. Things like:
"I am growing, even when it's hard."
"Progress, not perfection."
"I'm allowed to rest."

These visual reminders turn your journal into a friend — one that listens without judgment and helps you stay connected to yourself.

And if you prefer something creative, make it an art project! Use markers, washi tape, or printed cutouts. Decorate your "self-care corner" — a small space in your room where you keep your journal, a cozy blanket, a favorite book, or a candle. It's your personal recharge zone.

A printable checklist could also be something simple — a page where you mark each time you take care of yourself that week. It's not about perfection or checking every box — it's about noticing that you *showed up for yourself,* even in small ways.

Some weeks you might fill every space; others might feel emptier — and that's okay. Self-care isn't a race. It's a rhythm. There will be days you rest more, and days you accomplish more — both are valuable.

The point of a habit tracker isn't to keep score; it's to gently remind you that taking care of yourself is a lifelong relationship — one you get better at with time.

There's a quiet power in building routines that make you feel cared for. Over time, they become less about effort and more about instinct. You'll find yourself naturally drinking more water, saying kinder things to yourself, and creating balance in your days.

That's what self-care really is — not a list of things to do, but a way of living that honors who you are and what you need.

And here's something beautiful: the more you take care of yourself, the more you'll have to give to others. You'll notice you laugh more easily, handle stress with more grace, and shine a little brighter — not because life is perfect, but because *you're learning how to fill your own cup.*

So go ahead — design your routine, make it your own, and fill it with the things that make your heart smile. Because taking care of yourself isn't selfish — it's how you grow into the girl you were always meant to be.

<u>Chapter 6</u>

Handling Peer Pressure

and Social Media

The Pressure to Fit In

There's a moment in every girl's life when fitting in starts to feel like a full-time job. Maybe it's standing at your locker while your friends talk about something you don't really agree with, but you laugh anyway because you don't want to seem weird. Or maybe it's scrolling through social media late at night, comparing your life to perfectly edited photos and wondering, *Why doesn't my life look like that?*

That quiet pull — the one that whispers *just go along with it, don't stand out,* or *everyone else is doing it* — that's what peer pressure feels like. It's not always loud or obvious. Sometimes it's just a glance, a comment, or the feeling of being left out. But it can be powerful.

Fitting in is something everyone craves. It's human nature to want to belong. During puberty, when your body, emotions, and friendships are all changing at once, that desire becomes even stronger. You start to wonder where you fit, who likes you, and how you can make sure you're not "the odd one out."

But here's something most girls don't realize until later: belonging and fitting in are not the same thing.

Fitting in means changing yourself to be accepted by others. Belonging means being accepted *because* of who you truly are.

What Peer Pressure Really Looks Like

Peer pressure doesn't always look like a group of kids daring someone to do something bad. Sometimes, it's subtle — a friend rolling her eyes because you didn't join in on gossip, or someone teasing you for not watching the latest show everyone's talking about.

It can be pressure to look a certain way, to talk a certain way, or to do things that don't sit right with you — like pretending you're into things you're not, wearing clothes you're uncomfortable in, or even agreeing with opinions you don't believe in just to avoid being judged.

One of the trickiest parts is that peer pressure can come from people you like. Friends, classmates, teammates — even people who mean well can sometimes make you feel like you have to choose between their approval and your own comfort.

Social media adds another layer to all of this. Instead of just happening in the school hallway, peer pressure now shows up on screens — in likes, follows, filters, and group chats. It can make it feel like everyone's watching, and everyone's doing something you're not.

But what you see online is rarely the full story. Those photos you scroll through — the ones that seem perfect — are just snapshots. Behind every post is a real person with real insecurities, just like you.

When you start to compare yourself to others, you lose sight of your own path. You might start to think you need to change to keep up — change how you look, how you act, or what you say. But the truth is, the more you try to be like everyone else, the harder it becomes to remember who *you* are.

Common Social Challenges During Puberty

As you grow, your friendships, emotions, and sense of identity all evolve. That's normal — but it can also make social life feel like a rollercoaster.

There might be days when you feel left out of a group chat, or when your best friend seems to connect more with someone new. Maybe you notice that the friends you've known forever are changing — and so are you. That's part of growing up, but it can still hurt.

Sometimes you'll face tricky situations, like when a friend says something unkind about someone else and expects you to agree. Or when you're invited to join in on something you know isn't right — like spreading rumors or making fun of someone online. These moments test your character, even when no one else is watching.

It's okay to feel unsure in those moments. It doesn't mean you're weak or confused — it means you care. You want to do what's right without losing your friends, and that's a very real struggle. But the best friendships — the real ones — don't require you to compromise who you are.

Remember, confidence doesn't come from having everyone like you. It comes from liking *yourself*, even when others don't understand you yet.

How to Stay True to Yourself

When the world starts pulling you in different directions, staying true to yourself becomes one of the bravest things you can do.

The first step is listening — not to everyone else, but to that quiet voice inside you. The one that says *this doesn't feel right*, or *this isn't me*. That voice is your intuition, your inner compass. The more you trust it, the stronger it becomes.

You might not always get it right, and that's okay. There will be times you go along with something and realize afterward that it didn't make you feel good. Don't be hard on yourself — that's how you learn what aligns with your values. Growth happens when you pause, reflect, and decide differently next time.

It can help to remind yourself of what matters most to you. Is it kindness? Honesty? Respect? Being creative? Helping others? When you know your values, it becomes easier to make choices that fit your heart, not just your surroundings.

You'll start to notice a shift — instead of trying to fit in, you'll naturally attract people who respect you for who you are. You won't need to pretend anymore, because your energy will match the kind of friendships that feel genuine.

And yes, sometimes staying true to yourself means standing alone for a moment. That can feel scary, but those moments are where your strength grows. The people meant to be in your life will find their way back to you — and they'll respect you even more for standing firm.

One small but powerful habit is to ask yourself before making a decision: *Will this choice make me proud tomorrow?* That simple question can guide you in ways that surprise you.

You don't have to shout your boundaries or defend your every choice. Sometimes, quiet confidence is enough. A simple "No thanks," or "That's not for me," carries more power than you think.

You're not meant to blend in — you're meant to stand out in your own way.

The Strength in Being Yourself

The girls who seem the most confident aren't the ones who follow every trend — they're the ones who know what makes them feel authentic. They wear what they love, speak what they believe, and treat people with kindness because it feels right, not because it's popular.

The funny thing about being yourself is that it inspires others to do the same. When you choose honesty over pressure, you give your friends permission to be real too. Your courage ripples outward, creating space for authenticity and kindness in your circle.

So the next time you feel that pull — that quiet voice saying *maybe I should change to fit in* — pause. Take a breath. Ask yourself: *Would I rather be accepted for pretending, or respected for being real?*

You are allowed to outgrow friendships that don't make you feel valued. You're allowed to say no. You're allowed to choose yourself.

And you're allowed to be proud of the girl you're becoming — the one who doesn't just fit in, but stands out because she's genuine, grounded, and brave enough to stay true to her own heart.

Because at the end of the day, that's what makes you shine — not the number of followers you have, or how many people approve of you, but the confidence that comes from knowing who you are and honoring that truth every single day.

Online Confidence

It started with one photo.

Sophie had just downloaded a new app where everyone posted selfies and dance clips. She spent twenty minutes choosing a picture and then hesitated — should she use a filter? The filter made her skin smooth, her lashes longer, her smile brighter. When she looked at the edited version, she thought, *That's me, but better.*

She posted it. Within minutes, the likes started rolling in. Compliments, heart emojis, and "You're so pretty!" comments filled her screen. It felt amazing — for a while. But later that night, as she scrolled through other girls' posts, her heart sank. Their photos looked even more perfect. Their lives looked more exciting. Suddenly, Sophie didn't feel beautiful anymore. She felt like she needed to post again — but this time, even more edited, even more "perfect."

This is the hidden trap of social media: it can make you forget that the most beautiful thing about you is the part that doesn't need filters at all — your real, unedited self.

How to Stay Safe and Kind on Social Media

Social media can be fun, inspiring, and even empowering. It's where you can share your creativity, keep up with friends, and learn new things. But it's also a place that requires care — because every post, comment, and message becomes part of your online story.

Think of your social media presence like your digital reflection. The same way you'd take care of your body or your feelings, you also have to care for your online space.

Before you post, pause and ask yourself: *Would I feel good if someone showed this to my teacher, my parents, or my future self?* If the answer is yes, post with pride. If it's no, take a moment to rethink it.

Staying safe online also means protecting your privacy. It's okay to share parts of your life, but not everything needs to be public. Avoid sharing details like your school name, your address, or personal moments that could make you uncomfortable later. Remember — once something is online, it can be hard to take back.

Being kind online is just as important as being kind in person. The internet can make people forget there's a real person behind every screen. Before you comment or react, think about how your words might make someone feel. A kind message can brighten someone's whole day; a mean one can hurt more than you realize.

There's a special kind of confidence that comes from being someone who spreads positivity online. You don't need to post constantly to be seen — sometimes, just being supportive, encouraging, or real in your corner of the internet makes the biggest impact.

If you ever see negativity, bullying, or something that makes you uncomfortable, you don't have to join in or fight back. You can step away, block, or report it quietly. Protecting your peace is also self-care.

Social media should make you feel connected, not drained. If you ever find yourself scrolling and feeling sad, jealous, or left out, it's okay to take a break. Log off, breathe, and spend time in the real world — where laughter doesn't need likes, and friendships don't need filters.

The Truth About Filters and Perfection Online

There's a reason filters are so popular: they make us look "perfect." Smoother skin. Brighter eyes. Thinner faces. But here's the truth — those images don't show real life. They show a version of people that's been polished, edited, and sometimes completely transformed.

When you see a picture of someone who looks flawless, it's easy to compare yourself and feel like you're not enough. But what you're comparing yourself to isn't reality — it's a digital illusion.

Even the people you follow — influencers, celebrities, or classmates — don't wake up looking like their photos. They have insecurities, too. They have breakouts, bad hair days, and moments when they feel unsure of themselves. The difference is, you don't always see those moments online.

You might not realize how much editing goes into a single post: lighting adjustments, angles, retakes, filters, captions carefully written to seem effortless. It's not that these things are bad — creativity and self-expression are wonderful — but they can create a false standard that no one can live up to all the time.

That's why authenticity — being real — is so powerful. When you post something that's genuine, even if it's not "perfect," you remind others that it's okay to be human. You make space for honesty and connection instead of comparison.

There's beauty in imperfection. There's magic in laughter that's unposed, smiles that are crooked, and moments that are messy. The more real you are, the more you'll attract people who appreciate you for who you truly are — not just how you look.

And the next time you catch yourself thinking, *She's so much prettier than me,* or *I wish I looked like that,* remember: comparison is the thief of joy. You are already enough, just as you are — no filter required.

Digital Self-Worth: Being Proud of the Real You

Your worth isn't measured by how many followers you have or how many likes your photo gets. Those numbers don't define your beauty, your kindness, or your strength.

It's easy to forget that when social media turns everything into a competition — who looks best, who's most popular, who's "living their best life." But true self-worth comes from within. It's in how you treat people, how you handle challenges, and how you speak to yourself when no one's watching.

Imagine this: every time you post something online, it's like sending a message out into the world. What do you want that message to say? That you're chasing approval? Or that you're confident enough to be your authentic self?

Confidence online doesn't mean posting all the time. It means showing up with integrity — being real, respectful, and true to your values. It means knowing that your beauty and brilliance can't be captured in a single photo or measured in likes.

One way to build digital self-worth is to curate your feed with intention. Follow accounts that inspire you — creators who spread positivity, teach something meaningful, or make you feel seen and supported. Unfollow or mute anything that makes you feel small, pressured, or insecure.

Your online space should feel like a reflection of your best self — not your most "perfect" self, but your happiest, healthiest one.

There's something deeply freeing about realizing you don't have to prove yourself to anyone online. You can post less and live more. You can share what matters to you, not what's trending. You can laugh without recording it, make memories without posting them, and still feel completely whole.

When you let go of the need for validation, you make space for peace. You begin to understand that you are already enough — not because of how others see you, but because of how you choose to see yourself.

The real you — with your quirks, dreams, flaws, and all — is already worthy of love, respect, and celebration. The goal isn't to be the most "liked" version of yourself; it's to be the most *authentic* one.

The digital world is constantly changing, but one thing will always stay true: you have control over what kind of presence you create. You get to decide how you show up — with kindness, confidence, and courage.

So post the silly picture. Share your thoughts. Take breaks when you need to. Use your voice to spread light, not to chase approval. And never forget — behind every screen is a real person, just like you, trying to find their place in the world.

And when you look in the mirror — not through a filter, but with your real reflection — smile. Because that's the girl who deserves to be seen, online and off.

Saying "No" With Confidence

It's funny how such a small word — only two letters long — can sometimes feel like the hardest one to say. "No."

Maybe you've been in that moment: your friends want you to join in on something that makes you uncomfortable, but you laugh and nod anyway because you don't want to disappoint them. Or someone asks you for a favor when you're already exhausted, and you say yes because you don't want to seem rude.

Saying "no" can feel awkward, even scary. But here's the truth: every time you say "no" to something that doesn't feel right, you're actually saying "yes" — yes to your peace, yes to your boundaries, yes to who you are.

Confidence isn't about always being loud or fearless. It's about knowing yourself well enough to stand by your choices — even when it's uncomfortable. And learning to say "no" with grace and courage is one of the most powerful skills you can build as you grow into the amazing person you're becoming.

Setting Boundaries Without Guilt

Boundaries are like invisible fences that protect your emotional space. They help you decide what feels okay — and what doesn't. You already have them, even if you haven't called them by name. For example, maybe you don't like when someone borrows your things without asking, or you prefer quiet time after school before hanging out. Those preferences are your boundaries speaking up.

The challenge comes when others push against them. Maybe a friend teases you for not wanting to gossip, or someone makes you feel guilty for saying no. In those moments, it's easy to second-guess yourself — to wonder if you're being "too sensitive" or "too difficult."

But boundaries aren't about pushing people away; they're about protecting what matters most — your feelings, energy, and comfort. When you stand by them, you're not being mean. You're being respectful — to yourself and others.

You don't need to over-explain your reasons or apologize for setting limits. Sometimes, a simple "No, thank you" or "I'm not comfortable with that" is enough.

It's okay if your voice shakes a little the first few times you say it. It's okay if you rehearse what to say in your head before you do. What matters is that you're honoring yourself — and that kind of strength grows with practice.

And here's something beautiful: the people who truly care about you will respect your boundaries. They might not always understand them right away, but real friends don't want you to say yes when you really mean no.

You deserve to have relationships that feel balanced — where kindness and respect flow both ways.

Standing Firm in Your Values

There will be moments when you're tested — when doing what's right feels harder than doing what's popular. Maybe it's when your friends decide to exclude someone, and you're torn between joining in or speaking up. Or when you're pressured to look or act a certain way online to "fit in."

That's where your values come in.

Values are the beliefs that guide how you live your life — like kindness, honesty, respect, and compassion. They're the quiet compass that helps you make choices you can be proud of.

Standing firm in your values doesn't mean you'll never feel conflicted. It means that even when things get messy, you try to choose what aligns with your heart.

It takes real courage to stand apart sometimes. You might lose a few friendships along the way — especially with people who only liked the version of you that said yes to everything. But you'll gain something far more valuable: self-respect.

Think of your values like roots of a tree. When storms come — when gossip swirls, trends change, or people try to sway you — your roots keep you steady. You might bend, but you won't break.

You don't have to prove your values with long speeches or big actions. Often, quiet consistency says the most. When you keep showing up as yourself, even when it's hard, you become someone others trust and admire — not because you're perfect, but because you're real.

And remember: being confident in your values doesn't mean being stubborn or judgmental. It means being open-hearted but grounded. You can listen to others without losing yourself in their opinions. You can be kind without being a people-pleaser.

That's strength. That's maturity. And that's the kind of confidence that never fades.

When to Ask for Help and Who to Talk To

Even the strongest girls need support sometimes. Saying "no" and setting boundaries doesn't mean you have to face everything alone. In fact, one of the bravest things you can do is reach out when something feels too heavy to carry by yourself.

Maybe it's a situation that's confusing — like a friendship that suddenly feels toxic, or an online message that makes you uncomfortable. Maybe it's a secret that feels too big to handle on your own. Or maybe you're just tired of pretending you're fine when you're not.

You deserve to talk about it.

Start with someone you trust — a parent, older sibling, teacher, counselor, or close friend. You don't need to have the perfect words. You can start small, like saying, "Something's been bothering me," or "Can I talk to you about something that feels weird?"

It can feel scary to open up, especially if you're used to handling things yourself. But asking for help doesn't make you weak — it makes you wise. It shows you care about your wellbeing.

There's a quiet relief that comes with being heard — that moment when you realize you're not alone, that someone understands and wants to help.

And if you ever feel unsure about how to say no or where to draw a line, you can ask for advice. Trusted adults have been through their own versions of these moments. They can help you find words, strategies, and confidence to handle tricky situations with grace.

Sometimes, the best kind of help isn't advice at all — it's someone simply listening. The act of saying your worries out loud can lighten them, making them easier to manage.

If anyone ever makes you feel unsafe, pressured, or uncomfortable — online or offline — that's not a situation you need to handle alone. You have every right to speak up and seek support immediately.

You are never a burden for asking for help. You are a person who deserves to be cared for and protected.

The Power of "No"

The more you practice saying "no," the stronger and freer you'll feel. You'll start to realize that you don't owe everyone access to your time, your energy, or your emotions. You'll begin to see how beautiful it feels to make choices that truly align with who you are.

"No" can be gentle, calm, and kind — but it can also be firm. It doesn't need to come with guilt or endless explanations. Your feelings are reason enough.

Think about it: every time you say no to something that doesn't feel right, you make space for something that *does*. You say yes to your peace. Yes to your confidence. Yes to your authentic self.

And over time, "no" starts to sound less like rejection and more like respect — the kind that starts from within.

So take a breath the next time someone asks for something that doesn't sit right with you. Listen to that little voice inside — the one that knows what you need. Trust it. It's there for a reason.

Because being confident isn't about always saying yes. It's about knowing when to say no — and believing that your voice matters when you do.

<u>Chapter 7</u>

Embracing Change and

Becoming Your Best Self

E.J. Rico

Change Is Growth

If there's one thing every girl learns during puberty, it's that *nothing stays the same for long*. One day you look in the mirror and notice your body has changed. The next, your feelings seem louder, deeper, and more unpredictable than before. Even your friendships, interests, and dreams start to shift.

It can feel overwhelming — like you're standing on a bridge between who you were and who you're becoming. But here's the beautiful truth: change isn't something to fear. It's a sign that you're *growing*.

Every butterfly was once a caterpillar. Every tall tree started as a seed. Growth isn't always comfortable — but it's how everything in nature becomes what it's meant to be. And you, too, are unfolding into something incredible.

Why Change Helps You Grow Stronger

Sometimes, we wish things could stay the same forever — the same friends, the same routines, the same feelings of comfort and predictability. But if everything stayed the same, we'd never learn what we're capable of.

Think about it like this: every time you go through something new — whether it's starting at a different school, making new friends, or learning to handle tough emotions — you're building strength. Each challenge adds a little more confidence, a little more wisdom, a little more courage.

You may not notice it while it's happening, but every small change you face shapes you into someone stronger, kinder, and more resilient.

There's a moment in every girl's journey when she realizes that she's no longer the same person she was a year ago — or even a month ago. Maybe she's learned to speak up more. Maybe she's learned to take care of herself better. Maybe she's simply started to *understand* herself in a deeper way. That's growth in action.

And yes, growth can feel awkward at times — like when your clothes suddenly don't fit, your moods swing like a seesaw, or your body feels foreign. But those changes are your body's way of saying, *"I'm becoming stronger, healthier, and more capable."*

Even the parts that feel uncomfortable — like pimples, periods, or growing pains — are just your body doing its job. You're not falling apart; you're transforming.

The same goes for emotional growth. Every time you handle frustration, sadness, or nervousness with a little more patience or understanding, you're leveling up emotionally. You're learning that it's okay to feel deeply — and that feelings don't have to control you.

It's kind of like building muscles. The more you face new experiences — even the scary ones — the stronger you become. You're not meant to stay the same girl forever; you're meant to grow into the version of yourself that shines with confidence and courage.

Embracing Your Uniqueness as Your Power

Puberty can sometimes make you feel like you have to fit in — like there's one "right" way to look, act, or grow. You might catch yourself comparing your body to your friends', wondering why you're taller, shorter, curvier, or less so. You might even scroll through social media and think, *Why don't I look like her?*

But here's a truth that every strong girl learns eventually: your uniqueness isn't something to hide. It's your *superpower*.

The things that make you different are the things that make you unforgettable. The way you laugh, the way you think, the way you see the world — those are the colors that make your story special.

No one else has your exact combination of experiences, talents, or dreams. No one else will grow in the same way, at the same pace, or with the same light that you have. That's what makes you... *you*.

Imagine if every flower tried to look the same — if sunflowers wished they were roses, or daisies wanted to be tulips. The world would lose so much beauty. The same is true for people. The world doesn't need you to be like everyone else; it needs you to be the truest version of yourself.

Embracing your uniqueness also means giving yourself permission to grow at your own pace. Some girls get their period earlier; others later. Some develop faster, while others take more time. It's all normal — every timeline is different, and every timeline is beautiful.

You don't have to rush to become someone you're not ready to be. You don't have to copy someone else's journey. You just have to trust that where you are right now is exactly where you're meant to be.

Confidence doesn't come from perfection — it comes from self-acceptance. From standing in front of the mirror and saying, *"This is me, and I'm proud of who I'm becoming."*

That kind of confidence shines brighter than any trend or filter. It's quiet but powerful. It doesn't ask for permission — it simply exists.

And when you start seeing your differences not as flaws but as strengths, something magical happens: the things that once made you insecure become the things you love most about yourself.

How Every Girl's Journey Is Different (And That's Okay!)

There's no map for growing up. No two girls will take the exact same path, and that's what makes each story so special.

You might look around and see your friends changing — some seem to grow taller overnight, some get their periods early, and some still look the same for years. You might notice that your interests are shifting — what used to make you laugh now feels childish, or what used to scare you now excites you.

That's part of the adventure of becoming who you are.

It's easy to feel like you're "behind" or "different," but there's no finish line when it comes to growing up. Puberty isn't a race; it's a personal journey — one that unfolds in its own time, in its own way.

Even your emotions grow differently. Some girls feel confident right away, while others take longer to find their voice. Some love socializing; others prefer quiet reflection. Some feel ready for change, while others need time to adjust.

And guess what? Every single one of those paths is valid.

You're not supposed to have it all figured out. You're learning — and learning takes time.

Think of it like a sunrise. The light doesn't burst into the sky all at once; it grows slowly, beautifully, minute by minute, until the whole world glows. That's how you're growing too — quietly, steadily, in your own rhythm.

You might stumble, you might doubt yourself, you might have moments where you wish you could skip the awkward parts. But those are the exact moments shaping you into someone compassionate, wise, and resilient.

The best part of change is that it never stops teaching you. You'll keep learning about yourself — what you love, what you value, and what you want from life.

And one day, you'll look back and realize that all the changes you once worried about — the growth spurts, the mood swings, the doubts — were actually the building blocks of your strength.

You'll see that the girl who once questioned everything became the young woman who knows her worth, trusts her instincts, and embraces her individuality.

So when things feel uncertain or new, remind yourself: *This is growth.* You're not lost — you're expanding. You're not weird — you're original. You're not behind — you're right on time.

Every change, every challenge, every tiny step forward is shaping you into the person you're meant to be — not someone perfect, but someone real, grounded, and beautifully evolving.

Because growing up isn't about becoming someone else. It's about becoming more *you* than ever before.

Your Future Self

It's easy to get caught up in the *now* — the mirror reflections, the school days, the little dramas, the laughter that echoes through your group chat. But somewhere just ahead of you, there's another version of yourself waiting to meet you — one who's a little wiser, a little braver, and a lot more sure of who she is.

Your future self isn't some faraway stranger. She's already taking shape with every choice you make, every time you learn from a mistake, and every time you choose kindness — toward others and toward yourself.

You're not just growing *up*. You're growing *into* her.

Visualizing the Confident Girl You're Becoming

Close your eyes for a second and imagine her — your future self. Maybe she's standing in front of a mirror, her posture strong, her eyes bright with calm confidence. She knows who she is, what she values, and what makes her heart light up. She's not perfect, but she's real — and she's proud of herself.

Can you see her? Hear the way she talks to herself? Feel how comfortable she is in her own skin?

Now, here's a secret: you don't have to wait years to be that girl. You're already becoming her, one small step at a time.

Every time you choose to be honest instead of pretending, you're building her courage. Every time you take care of your body — brushing your teeth, eating well, resting, exercising — you're nurturing her strength. Every time you apologize, forgive, or try again after a bad day, you're shaping her resilience.

She's the sum of all the small, quiet moments when you showed up for yourself.

Sometimes, we think confidence just *appears* one day — like magic. But it doesn't. Confidence grows slowly, like sunlight through a window. It starts as a whisper — *You've got this* — and becomes a steady voice that says, *I can handle this, even if it's hard.*

Your future self will thank you for every time you chose to believe in yourself, even when doubt tried to take over. She'll thank you for every boundary you set, every time you said no to something that didn't feel right, and every time you said yes to something that scared you a little but helped you grow.

She's not someone you need to chase. She's someone you're building — piece by piece, choice by choice, day by day.

How to Keep Learning and Growing After Puberty

A lot of people talk about puberty as though it's an ending — like once it's over, the transformation is complete. But really, it's just the *beginning.*

Growing up doesn't stop when your body finishes changing. You'll keep learning about yourself for the rest of your life — and that's a wonderful thing.

Think about everything you've already learned: how to care for your body, how to handle emotions, how to speak up, how to choose friends who bring out your best. These lessons will keep evolving with you. You'll discover new things — how to manage stress, how to balance responsibilities, how to make choices that reflect who you are and who you want to become.

Life after puberty isn't about *having it all figured out.* It's about staying curious. About asking questions, making mistakes, and trying again.

You'll outgrow people, places, and habits that once fit perfectly. You'll discover passions that surprise you. You'll face challenges that test your patience and reveal your strength. And through it all, you'll realize that growth never ends — it just changes shape.

There will be moments when you miss the simplicity of being younger, and that's okay. Change often brings nostalgia. But it also brings new kinds of joy — independence, understanding, and purpose.

When you picture your future self, imagine someone who never stops learning — not just in school, but in life. Someone who stays open to new ideas, who listens, who explores, who learns from others and from her own heart.

One day, you'll look back and realize that every awkward, confusing, emotional moment of puberty taught you something valuable. Maybe it taught you patience. Maybe it taught you empathy. Maybe it simply taught you that you're stronger than you ever thought possible.

The lessons you're learning now are the foundation of the woman you'll become. And she'll carry them proudly — because they'll be the reason she stands tall, smiles easily, and walks through the world knowing she's enough.

Gratitude for Your Journey So Far

Take a deep breath and think about how far you've come.

The changes, the questions, the growing pains — you've navigated them all. Maybe not perfectly (no one does), but with courage. And that deserves appreciation.

Gratitude is a quiet kind of magic. It shifts your focus from what's missing to what's blooming. When you take time to notice how much you've grown, you realize you're doing better than you thought.

Remember the first time you faced something scary and did it anyway? Or the first time you stood up for yourself, even though your voice trembled? Those moments matter. They're proof that you're becoming someone capable and brave.

Being grateful for your journey doesn't mean pretending everything was easy. It means acknowledging the hard parts — the tears, the doubts, the uncomfortable changes — and honoring yourself for making it through.

Gratitude also teaches you to celebrate small wins. The mornings you woke up and chose to try again. The days you offered kindness when you didn't have to.

The moments you laughed with your friends until your stomach hurt. Those are victories, too.

You don't have to wait until you're "grown" to feel proud of yourself. You can celebrate your progress now.

Sometimes, writing it down helps. You might keep a small journal — not one filled with rules or pressure, just a few lines about what you're thankful for. It could be as simple as, "I'm grateful for my body for carrying me through today," or "I'm proud of myself for speaking up in class."

When you practice gratitude, you start to notice beauty in the everyday — in your morning routines, your friendships, your quiet moments. It helps you feel grounded, no matter how fast things change.

And maybe, when you look back years from now, you'll smile at how much you've grown — not just in height or maturity, but in self-love.

You'll realize that every phase — even the messy ones — was shaping you into the incredible person you were always meant to be.

Becoming Your Best Self

There's a version of you that's strong but gentle, confident but humble, curious and kind. She's not perfect — she doesn't need to be. She's simply growing, learning, evolving — always in progress, always becoming.

That's what being your "best self" really means. It's not about reaching some final, flawless version of yourself. It's about showing up every day with honesty, courage, and compassion — even when it's hard.

Your best self isn't just who you are when everything's going right. She's who you are when things fall apart — when you pick yourself back up, take a deep breath, and keep going anyway.

You're not growing into someone else. You're growing into *you*. The real you — the one who laughs loudly, loves deeply, and shines quietly.

So keep imagining her. Keep nurturing her. Keep talking kindly to her.

And when life changes again (because it always does), remember that change isn't something to fear — it's the bridge that carries you closer to your truest, brightest self.

Because every day, in ways both big and small, you're becoming the girl you were always meant to be — and that's something worth celebrating.

Keep Shining

There's something beautiful about realizing that *you* hold the power to shape who you want to become. Every choice you make — what you think, how you treat yourself, how you treat others — adds a little more light to your path. You're not waiting for someone else to hand you your sparkle. You're already carrying it inside you.

This chapter is about keeping that light alive — about setting gentle goals that help you grow, staying kind even when life tests your patience, and remembering that no matter what, you were born to shine in your own way.

Setting Personal Goals for Confidence, Health, and Happiness

You've come a long way on your journey through puberty — from learning about your changing body to understanding your emotions, friendships, and boundaries. Now, it's time to think about what comes next.

Setting personal goals isn't about being perfect or trying to control everything. It's about giving yourself direction — little milestones that remind you you're capable of growing intentionally and joyfully.

Maybe one of your goals is about *confidence*. Confidence isn't something you either have or don't; it's something you *build*. Think of it like a muscle that grows stronger with use. Maybe you want to raise your hand in class more often, share your opinions without shrinking back, or walk into a room without apologizing for taking up space. Every time you act with confidence, you teach your brain that you can trust yourself.

Another goal might be about *health*. Not the kind of health that's measured by numbers on a scale or clothing sizes — but the kind that makes you feel energized, balanced, and strong. Maybe it's drinking more water, going for walks, dancing in your room, or eating colorful foods that make you feel good from the inside out. Taking care of your body isn't a chore; it's an act of self-respect.

And then there's *happiness*. True happiness isn't about having everything figured out. It's about being present — noticing the small joys that fill your days: the smell of rain, the sound of laughter, the warmth of your favorite hoodie. It's about giving yourself permission to rest when you need to, to dream without limits, and to believe that you deserve joy, simply because you exist.

Sometimes, your goals will shift as you grow — and that's okay. You don't have to have a five-year plan. You just need to know what matters to you *right now*.

Because when you choose goals that align with your heart, you're already on the right path.

The trick isn't to chase perfection — it's to keep showing up for yourself, even in small ways. Growth isn't a straight line; it's a spiral. You'll revisit lessons, outgrow fears, and rediscover strength you didn't know you had.

You're not competing with anyone. The only person you need to be better than is the girl you were yesterday.

How to Stay Kind — to Yourself and Others

Kindness isn't weakness. It's one of the greatest forms of strength you can have. It takes courage to stay kind in a world that sometimes rewards being loud or cruel. But kindness is what makes you unforgettable — it's what softens hearts, builds friendships, and brings peace to your soul.

Start with *yourself.* You deserve the same compassion you offer others. Notice how you talk to yourself in your head — would you speak to a friend that way? If not, you can start changing the tone of your inner voice. Instead of "I messed up again," try "I'm learning, and that's okay." Instead of "I don't like how I look," try "I'm grateful for my body and what it allows me to do."

Self-kindness means letting yourself rest when you're tired, saying no when you're uncomfortable, and forgiving yourself when you make mistakes. It's realizing that growth takes time, and you don't have to rush it.

Being kind to others starts with empathy — seeing the world from someone else's eyes. Maybe a classmate who seems grumpy is just having a bad day. Maybe someone who's quiet isn't shy, but simply observing. When you pause to understand, kindness becomes your natural response.

But kindness doesn't mean you have to let people treat you poorly. It means choosing compassion *and* courage. You can be kind and still set boundaries. You can be gentle and still say no.

When you stay kind — even when it's hard — you create a ripple effect. Your smile might brighten someone's day. Your words might give someone hope. Your small acts of compassion might inspire someone else to pay it forward.

And most importantly, kindness keeps your heart light. It reminds you that goodness still exists, even on tough days.

A Final Pep Talk for Your Next Chapter in Life

If no one has told you this today, let it be me: *You're doing great.*

You've navigated so much change — physically, emotionally, socially — and you've done it with courage, curiosity, and heart. Even on the days when you felt unsure or overwhelmed, you kept going. That's bravery in its truest form.

As you step into your next chapter — whether it's high school, new friendships, or new responsibilities — remember that you don't have to have it all together. Life isn't about getting everything "right." It's about learning, trying, and growing.

There will be times when you question yourself, when things don't go as planned, or when you feel like you've lost your spark. In those moments, pause and breathe. Remember how far you've come. Remember the strength that lives inside you — the same strength that carried you through every change, every challenge, every victory so far.

And remember that your worth doesn't depend on your grades, your looks, your popularity, or your achievements. You are worthy *just as you are.*

When you feel unsure, go back to your inner compass — your values, your kindness, your intuition. They'll always guide you home.

And don't forget to dream big. The girl you are now is capable of amazing things. The world needs your ideas, your laughter, your empathy, your light. Whether you grow into an artist, a scientist, a teacher, a leader, or something entirely new — your impact will come from being authentically *you*.

You don't have to wait for permission to shine. You already have everything you need.

The confidence you've built, the self-awareness you've practiced, the empathy you've nurtured — these are your wings. They'll carry you through the next phases of your journey.

There will be bumps along the way — that's just part of life's rhythm. But don't let them dim your light. Every challenge you face will teach you something. Every setback will make you stronger. Every triumph, no matter how small, will remind you how capable you are.

You are not behind. You are not too much or not enough. You are exactly where you need to be.

So keep shining — not because you have to prove anything, but because light is who you are.

As you turn this page, imagine your future self smiling back at you, proud and grateful for the girl who dared to believe in herself. She's not waiting in the distance — she's here, in this moment, with every breath you take, every dream you chase, and every act of kindness you give.

Your journey doesn't end here; it's just beginning. Keep shining, beautiful girl. The world is brighter because you're in it.

Conclusion

You Did It! From Confusion to Confidence

You've made it all the way here — and I hope you know how incredible that is.

Maybe when you first opened this book, you felt a little nervous. Maybe you weren't sure what to expect... or even what to feel about all the changes happening inside and around you. And yet — here you are. Still curious. Still brave. Still growing.

That says something powerful about you.

Because growing up isn't just about what happens to your body — it's about how your *heart* stretches, too. It's learning how to trust yourself even when things feel messy or confusing. It's realizing that you can have questions, big emotions, and awkward moments — and still be completely, beautifully normal.

Remember those early chapters where we talked about the first signs of change? The flutter in your stomach when something new started? Back then, it might've felt like standing on the edge of a diving board, looking down and thinking, *Can I really do this?*

Now you know — yes, you can. You already are.

You've learned to listen to your body like it's a language — one that whispers, sometimes shouts, and always deserves to be heard. You've found ways to take care of yourself when things get uncomfortable, and you've learned how to talk about what used to feel too weird or embarrassing to say out loud. That's real growth.

And beyond the changes you can see, something even more beautiful is happening inside you: you're building a friendship with yourself.
That's the part most people forget to celebrate. But it's the secret to everything — friendships, confidence, happiness, even love.
Because when you treat yourself with kindness, the world starts to feel a little kinder too.

They'll still be days when you don't feel like your best self — and that's okay. Growing up doesn't mean never feeling lost again. It means knowing how to find your way back. And every chapter of your life from here on will give you a new chance to do that — to rediscover yourself in different ways.

Think of everything you've learned here as your personal toolkit — a mix of understanding, courage, and self-compassion. Use it when your friendships shift, when your emotions feel louder than usual, or when you just need a reminder that you're not alone in any of it.

And as you move forward — keep learning, keep asking questions, keep being curious about *you*. There's no single right way to grow up. There's only your way — your story, your pace, your rhythm.

One day, you'll look back and realize this was never just about puberty. It was about becoming you — the real you — the one who's learning to trust her own timing and glow in her own way.

So take a deep breath. Smile a little. And let yourself feel proud. Because this — this understanding, this courage, this gentle friendship with yourself — is what growing up is truly about.

You've got everything you need inside you already. And from here on out... it only gets brighter.

Epilogue

You know what's kind of amazing? This isn't the end. Not really. It's just a quiet pause — a deep breath before the next chapter of *your* story begins.

Because the truth is, you're going to keep changing. Your body will find new rhythms. Your emotions will keep teaching you things. You'll outgrow some moments, and grow beautifully into others. That's how life works — always moving, always unfolding, always surprising you in small, gentle ways.

If there's one thing I hope you carry with you, it's this: you don't have to have it all figured out. Nobody does. Growing up isn't about knowing everything — it's about *staying open*. Open to learning, to feeling, to becoming.

And the more you trust yourself, the easier it gets. You'll start to notice how strong you've become — how your thoughts are clearer, your voice louder, your heart softer in all the right ways.

The girl who started reading this book might've been full of questions. The one closing it now? She's full of possibilities.

So go out there — live, laugh, make mistakes, cry a little, then try again. Let yourself change. Let yourself shine. And whenever you feel unsure, come back to what you've learned here: you are growing exactly as you're meant to.

This story — your story — doesn't stop here. It keeps blooming in every step you take, every friendship you build, every brave little moment when you choose to be yourself.

Share Your Experience

If this book made you feel a little more understood... a little more confident about growing up... I'd love to hear from you.

Your thoughts mean more than you know — they help other girls find this guide and feel a little less alone, too.

Scan to leave a review

Or visit: http://bit.ly/3LagGFd

Thank you, truly, for being part of this journey — for showing up for yourself, for growing with kindness, and for reminding the world how beautiful change can be.

Acknowledgments

This book was born from countless conversations, quiet reflections, and the belief that every girl deserves to grow up with guidance that feels like a hug — not a lecture.

To the young readers who will hold this book in their hands: thank you. You are the heartbeat of these pages. Your questions, your curiosity, and your courage inspired every word.

To the parents, teachers, and mentors who nurture confidence and kindness in the next generation — your presence makes the world a gentler place.

To my family, who taught me empathy and patience, and to my friends who cheered me on during every late night of writing — your support turned this dream into something real.

And to those who have ever felt uncertain, unseen, or unworthy: this book was written for you. You are enough, just as you are. Always.

Author's Note

Dear Reader,

If you've made it this far, thank you — truly. Thank you for opening this book, for trusting me to walk beside you, and for allowing these pages to be a small part of your growing-up story.

When I first began writing *Girl's Guide to Puberty*, I didn't want it to sound like a textbook or a lecture. I wanted it to feel like a conversation — the kind you might have with someone who's been there, who remembers how confusing it all felt, but also how incredible it can be once you realize... you're becoming *you*.

This book was born from a simple wish: to make sure every girl knows that her changes — both seen and unseen — are something to celebrate, not fear. That it's okay to ask questions. It's okay to feel everything all at once. And it's okay not to have everything figured out yet.

Writing these chapters reminded me of my own journey — the uncertainty, the curiosity, the quiet courage that comes from learning who you are. And I hope, as you read, you felt that same courage growing inside you too.

So, from the bottom of my heart — thank you for your trust, your time, and your open heart.
Keep being curious. Keep being kind. And never forget: growing up isn't about changing who you are. It's about *coming home* to yourself, one chapter at a time.

With love,
E.J. Rico

About the Author

E.J. Rico is a writer, mentor, and advocate for emotional wellness and self-confidence in young people. Her passion for helping girls navigate the ups and downs of growing up began long before this book — in real conversations, small classroom talks, and countless moments of listening to stories that often went untold.

With a background in youth development and storytelling, E.J. believes that every young person deserves honest, kind guidance during life's most confusing changes. Her words are rooted in empathy — written not from a place of instruction, but from lived experience and deep care.

What makes her voice special is her ability to speak *to* readers, not *at* them. Through her writing, she builds trust — like a big sister, a friend, or that one adult who "gets it." She believes that confidence starts with understanding, and that understanding begins with honest conversation.

When she isn't writing, you'll find her journaling in quiet cafés, mentoring young girls, or hiking — the kind of long, thoughtful walks that turn into metaphors about life, change, and courage.

Girl's Guide to Puberty: 7 Friendly Ways to Understand Body Changes, Feelings, and Friendships During Puberty is more than her first book — it's her heartfelt letter to every girl who's ever felt unsure about growing up.

E.J. hopes that when readers finish this book, they don't just feel informed — they feel seen, supported, and beautifully human

Connect with E.J. Rico on Amazon

Want to read more books by **E.J. Rico**?
Scan below or visit my Amazon Author Page to explore new releases, updates, and upcoming projects made with the same warmth, honesty, and heart.

Or visit:
http://amazon.com/author/ej_rico77

Thank you for reading — and for growing with me.

E.J. Rico

The Light Within You

Somewhere inside you, there's a steady glow — quiet, constant, and real. It doesn't fade when life gets hard. It doesn't disappear when you doubt yourself. It's your light — your confidence, your compassion, your courage.

As you move beyond these pages and into your next adventures, carry that light with you. Let it guide you through new experiences, friendships, and dreams.

You don't have to know everything yet. You don't have to be anyone other than who you already are. All you need is the willingness to keep learning, to stay open, and to keep growing — even when things feel uncertain.

There will be days when you'll question if you're enough. Remember this moment. Remember how far you've come — the lessons you've learned, the feelings you've explored, the strength you've built. You are already enough.

The truth is, you were never meant to fit into someone else's idea of perfection. You were meant to shine as *yourself*.

So keep being curious. Keep being brave. Keep choosing kindness — especially toward yourself.

And every once in a while, look back and whisper to your younger self: *You did it. You grew. You bloomed.*

Because even though this book ends here, your story — your incredible, one-of-a-kind story — is only beginning.

Shine on, beautiful girl.
The world is waiting for your light.

Praise for *Girl's Guide to Puberty*

"This book feels like a friend — the kind who listens without judgment and always knows what to say. My daughter didn't just read it; she *hugged* it."
— *Maria S., parent of a 12-year-old*

"I wish I had this book when I was growing up. E.J. Rico speaks with so much heart — turning what could be awkward or confusing into something beautiful, brave, and normal."
— *Dr. Hannah Lee, Adolescent Health Educator*

"Finally, a puberty guide that doesn't talk *at* girls but *with* them. Every chapter feels like a warm conversation — honest, funny, and kind."
— *Tessa R., middle school counselor*

"As a teacher, I've seen so many students light up after reading this. It gives them language for what they're feeling — and permission to be gentle

with themselves."
— *K. Delacruz, Educator*

"*Girl's Guide to Puberty* reminds us that growing up is not something to fear — it's something to celebrate. My teen and I read it together, and it opened conversations we'd been avoiding for years."
— *L. Ramirez, parent*

"This book should be in every school library. It's science, soul, and sisterhood — all wrapped into one comforting read."
— *Youth Wellness Review Panel, 2025*

"E.J. Rico doesn't just teach — she understands. And that's what makes this book so special."
— *Reader Review, verified on Amazon*

Printed in Dunstable, United Kingdom

71377678R00100